# Venice to London

## Odyssey of Medieval European Banking

Sumera Khan

Venice to London

THE VISION CAPITAL
A FinTech Company in MEASA
Co-Founded by the Author

To my father and to my husband, for desiring to have a pen in my hand.

# ACKNOWLEDGMENTS

I acknowledge the incomparable service of Satoshi Nakamoto who shaped the Modern Era of Finance through conceiving Blockchain, and empowering people of common rank to be bankers, financiers not just clerks and pencil-pushers for *"to-big-to-fail"*, and create what is improbable otherwise for us.

Venice to London

# CONTENTS

# PREFACE

It was 2008, when working for a large bank, and studying Economics for masters', I started to take deeper interest upon the subject of research into the origin of money, credit, finance and banking. I requested the panel to grant me the subject of "Odyssey of European Banking" for my thesis, but I was turned down for unforeseen reasons. I did not give up and started my research from Indus-Valley civilization, and travelled in Far East, Middle East, CIS, MENA, and Europe for eight years, following the footsteps for Finance and taking notes.

Venice to London is the anecdote of banking and bankers in Europe, particularly for the new wave of bankers and financiers who are changing the course of Finance and Banking through disruptive technologies, new ideas and concepts. It is for the P2P insurance providers, robo-advising technology developers, FinTech entrepreneurs, and Venture Capitalists who are speeding to fund the Financial Technology startups across Europe.

Brexit is unquestionably a momentous event in the history of Banking and Finance, when century's long monopoly of the City of London upon global finance has shifted the ground to other places and London banks are declaring to relocate their houses from the City to other countries. The advent of printing press made it possible to publish a lot about the bankers and banks in nineteenth and twenty first century, but the occupation of Banking and bankers is still in the darkness before nineteenth century.

Several students of Banking and Finance are aware of the name of *The Bank of Venice* but they are unaware of the events surrounding the conception, evolution, and downfall of the Bank of Venice, even many does not discern that it was not actually a Bank of Venice but it was a couple of banks, with different names and purposes. Little is known about the mechanisms, and commerce of the earlier banks of Europe. The importance of this knowledge increased, particularly in the post-financial crisis world, when Finance is changing rapidly from being concentrated into a few hands to the billions of hands, carrying mobile devices around the world.

In 2017, even students with software skills are creating banking and financial institutions every day, they are transforming the trade of stocks, commodities and other financial instruments from human beings to the machines, and in such a world, where disruption is out of hands, the knowledge for everybody about the banking, the skills of banking and financing has never been essential like today.

World War II and Bretton Wood conference is the birth of Modern Finance and Banking. The conference of representatives of forty-five nations at Bretton Wood in July 1944, under the leadership of **John Maynard Keynes** was not about the creation of future course of global economy but I believe it was about the channelizing excess American resources through United Kingdom as dealer, mostly to European nations, and then to their colonies and allies. The economic state of Europe, at times, cannot be articulated better than the words of eminent historian, Basil Liddle Heart;

> The Western Allies entered that war with a two-fold object. The immediate purpose was to fulfil their promise to preserve the independence of Poland. The ultimate purpose was to remove a potential menace to themselves, and thus ensure

their own security. In the outcome, they failed in both purposes. Not only did they fail to prevent Poland from being overcome in the first place, and partitioned between Germany and Russia, but after six years of war which ended in apparent victory they were forced to acquiesce in Russia's domination of Poland — abandoning their pledges to the Poles who had fought on their side.

At the same time, all the effort that was put into the destruction of Hitlerite Germany resulted in a Europe so devastated and weakened in the process that its power of resistance was much reduced in the face of a fresh and greater menace — and Britain, in common with her European neighbours, had become a poor dependent of the United States.

Two wars with in half a century has scorched down Europe to ashes and the need of everything was never seen before. At the end of WWII, USSR decided to wall their winnings of war from the rest of the world, while Americans took the opportunity to export its surplus resources to the penurious, hence the era of "freedom and democracy" began. The City of London became the gateway of the transfers to the Europe from America, off course, for cumbersome fees and commissions. For the purpose of understanding, I name the surplus resources as "wealth" that includes everything, from Wheat to Cash, currency, goods and services.

When Europe was fighting wars, Americans were working and producing the wealth in factories and offices, which in turn was being converted into Dollar bills at Banks and mints. To buy or borrow the wealth, Europe needed medium of exchange for the American factories and offices, and European nations had to exchange their currencies with American Dollars so that they can buy the American goods and services.

WWII was the end of Great Britain and birth of United Kingdom. Great Britain died in Dunkirk, despite the fact that she was still occupying India, much of Africa and the Middle East. The death of Great Britain is chronicled by *Robert Skidelsky*, the best-known profiler of John Maynard Keynes in these words;

> "Churchill fought to preserve Britain and its empire against Nazi Germany; Keynes fought to preserve Britain as a Great Power against the United States. The war against Germany was won; but in its effort to win it, Britain spent its resources so heavily that it was destined to lose both its Empire and its Great Power status."

The interests of industrial investors and financial bankers often conflict too. Financiers, for instance, tend to like high interest rates, from which they can derive considerable income, while industrialists want low interest rates, to curb their costs. Brexit – is perhaps the most important historical event of 2017, when officially United Kingdom, once the Great Britain falls back to an Island, and gigantic journey of its banking houses to other nations is bewildering. For centuries, the City has ruled the world of finance, and the London bankers, always ruled the world with her immense power of credit, through lead in occupation of finance.

Recently, since Satoshi Nakamoto, an unknown entity, in October 2008, published a paper suggesting a digital currency, we now know as Bitcoin. It was foundation of the future of Finance, now branded as FinTech or Financial Technology, and it is taking over the business of Financial Services, including banking, payments, exchanges, investments, Financial Advisory etc. Without any shadow of doubt, the old banking is diminishing and rapidly moving from human beings to machines. This book is tale of those centuries and the world of finance, when the diminishing Banking was born, flourished, travelled from the shores and swamps of Venice to the city of London.

The world of banking and finance, rapidly changed in post-global financial crisis of 2008-09, and emergence of FinTech. This book is carved definitely for the publicists, supporters and developers of Financial Technology to learn how the disruptive enterprises and ingenuities in the world of banking and finance made gaffes, faced hurdles, squandered the opportunities, and changed the history. There is a lot to learn from the history, before resolving to start a FinTech company, a lot to learn from the fates of people like *William Paterson*, who founded the Bank of England, the early Scotch bankers and the Black Monday, before being too overwhelmed by the promises of crowd funding and digital banks.

**Sumera Khan**

Dubai, UAE.

Email: sumerakhanlodhi@yahoo.com

Figure 1 Painting of Medieval moneylenders and pawnbrokers in the northern city states of Italy during the Renaissance

Painting of Medieval moneylenders and pawnbrokers in the northern city states of Italy during the Renaissance

# INSTITUTION OF BANKING IN EUROPE

The first *banco* or bench in Europe was created in 808 A.D. by *Lombard Jews* in Italy. The name bank is resulting from *banco*, a bench, which was created in the market place for the exchange of money[1]. These *bancos* was kept by the *Lombard Jews* in the markets. When a banker failed, his bench was broken by the populace; and from this circumstance we have the term *"bank-rupt"*. From earliest European history of Banking, a banker is a dealer in money, currency, coin, cash and credit in any form and shape. Banking, as we know today, has emerged and progressed through thousands of years and hundreds of civilizations, starting from the oldest societies of Indus-Valley, itinerant towards Mesopotamia, and later to Byzantium. From Byzantium, the Banking attained Roman Empire, and thrived there, largely into Italian city states.

During thirteenth and fourteenth century AD, the money-changers in Venice transitioning from merchants to bankers, in similar manner to that by which the merchants in Amsterdam a couple of centuries later, and further later the London goldsmiths, became bankers. From the High Middle Ages ca. 1400 to the foundation of the *Bank of England* in 1694, the meaning of "money" oscillated from virtual credit and private "currencies," to securities, to bullion, and back again, in just three hundred years.

The earliest public bank established in modem Europe was that of Venice, which was founded in 1157. It started from a

---

[1] Dictionary of dates, and universal reference, By Joseph Timothy Haydn, 1841.

loan, the State raised during the great war of the Republic with the Greek empire (1156-71). To fight the crisis, contributions as loans were demanded from the wealthy citizens, and the Chamber of Loans— *Camera degl' imprestiti* —was established to manage the collected loans, and of guaranteeing the payment of four percent interest, to the creditors. Subsequently, the creditors were incorporated in a Joint stock company, and this was foundation of what was later known as the Bank of Venice.

The private banking in Venice began as an accessory of the business of the *campsores*, or foreign exchange brokers. In a city having a motely trade with many countries, these dealers necessarily held an imperative place, close to the stream of payments which was relentlessly in motion. As early as 1270 it was reasoned necessary to entail them to give sanctuary to the government as the condition of carrying on their business, but it is not revealed that they were then receiving deposits. Governing provision of banking, in 1445, after nearly two centuries, requisite the bankers to be present daily for a certain number of hours. Half a century later, the directive in Venice was reading;

- It shall be free for everyone to accept or not accept a credit in bank (*partida de banco*) for contracts made heretofore; but this shall not be refused for those made hereafter, unless by express agreement it shall have been declared that payment shall be made outside of bank.
- Credit in bank shall not be written off to any one for any amount in his absence; but credits shall be written with both parties present.
- Bankers, as aforesaid, must pay, to those who wish, in cash at once and in hand their money in good and heavy gold, or good moneys at the market rates, or rates current at our offices; and, if any should refuse, they shall be subject to the

penalty of twenty-five ducats, and the proveditor[2] then present shall none the less make them pay.

It is appropriate to show that in 1584 the allocation of credit had long been an important means of payment. The progression saved the need and labour of counting coin and of its labor-intensive conveyance in every transaction. The coin itself had been deposited as the bedrock of the credit, and was to be compensated on delivery: the conception of credit without such deposit was in his view a misuse; but payments could be made by the transfer of the right of the depositor to demand, with such facility as to enable traders to carry on dealings to a magnitude otherwise impossible. *"Buyer and seller are satisfied in a moment, while the pen moves over the page: whereas a day would not be enough to complete the contract for a great mass of merchandise by counting a great number of coins,"* chronicled *Tommaso Contarini.* It was to secure the gain of payment in this expedient system, without the risks of secluded mismanagement, that, as we shall see, the public bank was subsequently established.

In 1403, already an act was passed banning any banker to ship or send away by land either goods or money beyond the amount of one and a half times the loans which he might have made to the republic. Alternatively, trade with the Levant, the western trade, corn, exchange, the accommodation of friends, the purchase of lands and houses, were typical classes of a banker's investments in that age. Loans to individuals had some place among the bankers' use of capital is shown by an act of

---

[2] A functionary in the Venetian republic having oversight of public services and government of provinces or acting as military adviser.

1467, limiting to ten ducats the amount which could be on loan to any person upon a single commitment[3].

The historic papers reveal the records and actions of the Venetian Senate of 1584 and 1587, which established the first public bank in Venice, *Banco di Rialto*; and numerous other proceedings regulating the structure of the bank, for instance, a speech made in the Senate, in 1584, by *Tommaso Contarini*, in favor of establishing a public bank; and a speech, by an unknown senator, opposing such an institution. These are published by Professor Elia Lattes in 1869.

It is though uncertain when the merchant banks of Venice started to manipulate the credit, and when they began the practice of the modern system of issue. The idea must have come soon after deposits became common. We learn from *Contarini* that in the sixteenth century, a banker can issue credit to his friends without the actual deposit, simply by writing a brief entry of credit. The banker could grant himself credit to buy fine furniture and ornaments by just writing two lines in his books, and can buy estates or donate any sum without any actual costs. This was the beginning of *fiat system of credit and currency*, and fabrication of records and ledger entries. The popularity of deposit accounts with Banks, provided the bankers with authority needed, and they were quick to exploit it in their favor by swindles. The creation of fiat currency is to the credit of Venetian merchant banks and bankers.

In those old days, it was not so easy to go unnoticed with such manipulations and fiddles. When, in 1445, the bankers were

---

[3] *Nuova Antologia*, January, 1871, p. 205. The loans noted by Ferrara are those mentioned in scattered documents, and it is certain that their amount is far below the real total.

required to be present for business diurnal, at least two hours in the morning and two after dinner, instead of presenting themselves only *quando et quanto voleno*, we may be sure that the Senate planned, among other things, to provide for depositors who might wish to draw out their money. Then prerequisite in 1467 that bankers should show to any person the books containing his accounts and balances, *rationes et resta sua*; and later the strict provision in 1523 that the bankers should have ready on the counter, *sopra li banchi tenir conveniente*, the money for making their payments in full and must count it out publicly *sopra il banco* or be responsible for any deficiency sworn to by the beneficiary, these requirements may have been directed against debtors eluding payment either from humiliation or fraud.

The repeated increase of the security to be given by bankers, which in 1523 had risen to 25,000 ducats; the summary jurisdiction over questions between bankers and depositors, given, by various acts from 1421 to 1523, to designated public officers; and other protections into the detail of which it is incredible to enter, all show that the republic was painfully aware that swift payment was not always the first purpose of the Venetian banker. How much the republic achieved by its efforts to regulate the banks is uncertain.

With a system of manipulation, sham fiat credit fabrication, and banking obligations on which payment is evaded or deferred, fall is an expected outcome. There is pretext to infer from the law of 1421 that this malevolent had then revealed itself; for the law explains that, as money cannot be drawn from the banks, there is a practice of selling credits held against them, with great injury to the state. The malevolent appears more clearly in 1523, when the law states that the banks shall make their payments without deduction for cash, *far li pagamenti integri et senza alcuna diminuzione*, and also prevents the buying or trade of money with bank credits, - a proscription which infers a difference in value, and hence a fall of the credit.

But the *"Ordinationes circa bancos "*of 1526 declare in so many words that the exaction practiced by the bankers upon those who wished for money had then reduced the bank credit twenty percent below the extent of cash. The cure applied was forceful. The number of the *sopra banchi* already in office as inspectors of the banks was amplified, so as to give one for each bank, their attendance day by day during banking hours was necessary, and substantial authorities were given to them. Dealings in bank credit with an agio for cash, *con alcun Itaza*, were then outlawed.

It was enforced that exchange should be sold at one price, whether for cash in hand or in bank, and that payments for goods or for other cause should be made in the same way, the bank credit to be taken, if at all, on the equilibrium of cash, *ducat for ducat*, the bankers being at the same time required under penalty to uphold their payments in cash. In the prelude of a law relating to money-changing passed in 1528, it is declaimed that these requirements had brought the bank ducat and cash to equality of value. Two years later a law respecting bills of exchange makes the same recital, but adds that at the Lyons fair bills had been drawn payable in bank with a difference of two and a half percent, and therefore requires that bills drawn payable in bank shall be settled at the rates current for bills made payable in cash.

Details of the *failure of several banks* have been noted by Ferrara,[4] the cases of the *Soranzi, Garzoni,* and *Lippomani* being the most remarkable. The winter of 1498-99, when the two-latter failed and the *Pisani* had in consequence to meet a run by depositors looks to have been a season of anxiety in Rialto. There are also indications of serious trouble not far from 1523. In 1584 came the failure of the house of *Pisani* and *Tiepolo* for 500,000 ducats, and this event apparently brought private banking in Venice to its end. Its history, if we may judge from the derelict, was a tale of recurrent catastrophe; and yet it must be reminisced that the events which appear to us now as parts of a single picture were, in fact, spread over the greater part of three centuries, during which the Venetian public continued to delegate its securities to the private banks.

A debate in, the Venetian Senate which, in a few months after the fiasco of Pisani and Tiepolo, ended in the act of December, 1584, for the creation of a public bank, to be called the *Banco della Piazza di Rialto*. This act was annulled in the following April, in consequence of tough hostility; and it would appear that the city was left for the next three years without any bank, either public or private, to the great misperception and injury of its business. The act of April 11, 1587, at last established a bank of deposit, sometimes called the *Banco di Rialto*, and sometimes the *Banco della Piazza*[5]. The acts of 1584 and 1587 varied in some noteworthy details, but they agreed in their main purpose of granting to a public institution the deposit business so long retained by the private bankers; and we can therefore

---

[4] A lively account of this run, given by Malpiero and cited by Ferrara, may be found in the *Archivio Storico*, Ser. I., vol. vii. p. 715.

[5] The acts of 1584 and 1587 are given in full by Lattes, pp. 101 and 109.

conveniently pivot our attention now to the act of 1587, as expressing the meaning of the revolution in Venetian banking which took place in 1584.[6]

The act of 1587, after recounting the troubles resulting from the devastation of the private banks, the inordinate necessity of a bank of some kind, and the conclusion that private banks could not supply the demand, establishes *Banco de scritta* for three years, to be placed under the charge of a governor elected by the Senate for the same term, and under the inspection of the *Proveditori soprabanchi*. The bank was required to receive all cash deposits offered in good and contemporary money; the money was to remain always subject to call, *sempre pronto a requisition di creditors*; transfer in bank could be made, but only in the presence of the depositor or by his written permission wedged in the office of the *soprabanchi*; no transfer could be made in outright, but credit must be given in account to the transferee at the same time that the transfer was withdrawn; and, finally, the expenses of the institution were to be met by means of the duties on imported goods.

In December, 1593, a further act provided that all bills of exchange should thereafter be paid by transfers in bank only. It

---

[6] Morosini, in his *Historta Veneta*, under 1587, says "*Negotia torum quoque incommodo subvenire decretum, qui, apud privatos mensarios pecunia deposita, eorum fraude, avaritia, crebrisque decoctionibus ingentes jacturas damnaque patiebantur; ex quo publicis etiam redditibus haud parva detrimental accedebant. Itaque lex lata in Senatu, ut publica mensa erigere tur, in qua tuto singuli argentum aurumque adservarent; ei Gubernator prae ficeretur, qui rite atque ex ordine cuncta administranda curaret; id munus Francisco Gradenico primum tributum.*" But Morosini takes no note of the establishment of the Banco del Giro in 1619, and perhaps supposed that bank to be the same as the "*mensa* "of 1587.

is apparent from these provisions that the *Bank of the Rialto* was not a bank in the modern sense, as the private banks superseded by it had been. The republic wisely declined to commence the investment of the funds delegated to it, pursued no profit from the use of its credit, and, in short, merely undertook to keep the money of depositors in safety, and to pay it out or transfer it to others at the necessity of the holder. At a given moment the depositors might even draw out the whole of the cash, in full consummation of their entitlements, if they chose, and nobody would be any the worse[7]. Certain roles of the private banks were thus selected and made the work of the new institution, and the rest were omitted. It is clear, then, that this development of the Venetian public bank from the business carried on in private hands had no possible relation to any public debt or to any use which the state might be able to make of the coins deposited with it.

The *Act of 1584* had banned the formation of private banks, *restando nell' avenire pro htibito del titto a' partieolari il levar pii' banchi*; but this act being annulled, and the act of 1587 containing no such embargo, the formation of private banks may be said to have become probable, although for many years bankers and banks were not expected to appear on the horizon. But in February, 1596-97, the Senate, after reciting the cul-de-sac of meeting all the needs of commerce by a solo bank, gave to Dionisio Contarini, who had served as governor of the public

---

[7] It is worth noting that the governor of the bank was forbidden under heavy penalties to traffic in, use, or lend any of its moneys. Lattes, p. 110. Contarini's discussion as to what might happen in case of war, and his assertion of the ability of the bank to pay everything on demand, *tanto sarh il dar, quanto l' haver*, is important as showing that commercial and not fiscal convenience was the purpose of the undertaking. See Lattes, p. 137.

bank, permission to start a private bank for six years. The banker bound himself to give security to an extent declared to be unexampled, and to supply the mint annually with an agreed quantity of gold and silver.

All his receipts and payments were to be in good money of lawful weight, he was to undertake no public contract for merchandise, and payments offered by transfer upon his accounts were to be receivable only at the pleasure of the payee. Nothing more has yet been brought to notice respecting Contarini's bank; but in 1619 the Senate again gave a companion to the Bank of the Rialto by the act of May 3, creating the famous *Banco del Giro*, - a public bank whose foundation is so often said to date from the twelfth century. The two banks, organized separately, but with similar rules, continued to work side by side until 1637, when the *Bank of the Rialto* was superseded as result of the acquisition of its business by the Bancogiro; [8] and the latter was then left as the sole denizen of the field[9].

The conditions under which the *Banco del Giro* was established are stated in general terms in the introduction of the act. *Giovanni Vendramin* had contracted to supply to the Venetian mint a large amount of silver, in bulk or in Spanish

---

[8] Rezasco, who made a diligent search in the Venetian archives for matter relating to the two public banks, cites the order abolishing the Bank of the Rialto as dated January 2, 1637. *Dizionario di Linguaggio Italiano Storico ed Amministrativo*, p. 85.

[9] The Banco del Giro was so named, as has often been explained, because of the continual movement of credit by transfer from one depositor to another. The name distinguished the bank from the Banco della Piazza, but the practice referred to by it was in no way peculiar to the new bank, as has been shown already.

reales (*The silver real, Spanish: real de plata*) and to receive payment, one-half in coin or in bank credit, and the other half in gold, either coined or in bars; and, as the rate at which he supplied the silver was low, the republic agreed to make him a large loan in bank credit. At the same time there were traders, to whom the republic was indebted for goods and for bills of exchange, who had received guarantees upon the mint and other public offices, the collections upon which were slow and embarrassed by official forms.

To make a prompt settlement with Vendramin and with the other creditors, the new bank was created, and placed in charge of an officer called the *Depositario del Banco del Giro*; and the creditors were paid by being credited with deposits on its books. To enable the bank to meet the request for payment to which it was thus exposed, a large sum in reals received from Vendramin was exchanged at the *Banco di Rialto* for current money; and this, with coin struck from silver in bulk supplied under Vendramin's contract, was placed in the *Banco del Giro*, to the extent of 150,000 ducats, as a reserve. It was also provided that payments of 10,000 ducats per month (increased soon afterwards to 30,000 ducats) should be transferred from the mint to the bank, until the sum of 500,0410 ducats, the amount of the payments to be made to public creditors, should be covered[10].

---

[10] These transactions can be made out with reasonable clearness from the preamble and the last four sections of the act of 1619 establishing the bank. An account is given of them by Rezasco, p. 82, with some details as to Vendra min's contract obtained by examination of the original. There is also a brief account given in a short memoir on the public banks, written near the end of the seventeenth century by the senator Bernardo Trevisan, and published under the title of

**Venetian Gold Ducat**

---

Informazione per il Banco del Giro in Vigano's translation from Sonnleithner, La Scienza del Commercio, p. 293.

The credit of the bank was to be persistent, therefore, not only by the good faith and policy of the republic, but ultimately by the actual presence of all the money which the

**Spanish colonial real**

credit might represent. This system contained the least possible mystery, either as regards theory or practical operation; and the *Bancogiro* would have been simply a second *Bank of the Rialto* but for the fact that the debts of the republic to Vendrarnin and the other public creditors were the reason for its creation.

As it was, instead of opening for business with neither obligations nor cash on hand, as a simple bank of deposit might have opened, the *Bancogiro* began with a substantial liability upon its books to assure creditors of the state, and with a considerable resource in cash, which the state agreed to fill up to the full amount of the liability. This state of affairs presented some elucidation for the belief that the *Bank of Venice* was originally a public debt; and, taking into account further the fact that the *Banco del Giro* superseded the *Banco di Rialto* so effectively that the date of its own formation was, as it were, immersed, and that the transfer of deposits, the *giro* practiced by both, was their best known characteristic, and had also been the practice of private bankers for an unknown period, we can see the possible growth of the legend which finally assigned to the Bank of Venice a life of about six centuries.

For the present purpose, at any rate, it is enough to say that the republic did not find it easy to carry on the business of the bank in the regular course expected by the law. The responsibility to fill up the reserve of the bank by monthly payments was, in effect, a liability to pay off a public debt at that rate from revenue; and, this being found difficult, fresh creations of liability put off the time for effecting the payments. In 1630, the closing of the bank was determined upon, and the raising of the money needed for this purpose was provided for; but some changes in activities - the effect probably of the breaking out of the war in Candia in 1631 - caused this plan to be abandoned. The bank kept on with varying success and credit; and in 1650 money was again raised to cover in part the public debt and thus to place the establishment on a firmer basis.

During all this earlier part of its history, however, the bank probably suffered as much from disorderly management as from the inability of the government to clear off its debt. Notwithstanding the elaborate regulations prescribed by law to insure against official malfeasance, frequent irregularities and frauds appear to have occurred; and several revisions of the regulations had to be made to check the negligence of responsible officers. In 1662, a great fraud committed by a book keeper was discovered; and it is to this culmination of malevolent in the management of the bank that the revision of its regulations in 1663 was due. The new code then published is filled with such minute provisions against neglect and misconduct, and contains such frequent references to abuses and fraud, as to give the impression of a constant struggle with unfaithful or dis honest servants.

The eighteenth century saw the cash office of the bank closed and specie payments postponed, from 1717 to 1739, as a consequence of the wars in which the declining republic was engaged for many years. The credit of the bank fell during this period, but recovered when the cash office was resurrected by order of the Senate in 1739; and thereafter the commercial journalists treat the bank as a solid and important establishment until the breaking out of the wars of the French Revolution. The humiliation of the republic by 1797 had led to such drafts on the cash of the bank that, with a deposit of nearly 1,500,000 ducats, the reserve was reduced to a little over 522,000 ducats.

The bank, however, survived the occupation of Venice by the French; and when, under the treaty of *Campo Formio* in October, 1797, the Venetian republic was extinguished and the city was given to Austria, an effort was made to reinstate the credit of the institution by creating a recovery fund, *fondo di Amortizazione*, supported by a stamp duty on bills of exchange, bills of lading, and policies of marine insurance[11] and later by other revenues.

The deficit was for a time reduced; but the Austrian administration found its own needs urgent and the coffers of the bank tempting, and in 1804 the deficit had again risen, according to *Rezasco*, to nearly 1,280,000 ducats. The *Fiscal deputato al Banco giro* reported at some length in January, 1805, upon some reforms for the benefit of the redemption fund. But the defeat of the Austrians at Austerlitz and the treaty of Presburg in December, 1805, brought Venice under the French domination; and in July, 1806, Napoleon issued his decree for the liquidation

---

[11] Proclamation by Count de Walis, imperial commandant, October, 1798.

of the debts of the *Bancogiro*, allowing for one-fourth of the amount scrip receivable for acquisitions of public property, and registering the other three-fourths in the public debt called the *Monte Napoleone*. This hit, by a heavy hand, closed a significant chapter in economic history.

It is important to note the effect produced by the suspensions of payment, which, as has been learnt, occurred several times, beginning with perhaps more than one such period during the war of Candia [12] between 1631 and 1669. In order to do this, however, we must fleetingly consider the nature of the currency used by the bank. *The ducat* in which the bank kept its accounts was twenty percent higher in value than the actual ducats in circulation, or, in other words, that the bank used a money of account which bore this premium when rated in current money [13]. The ducat *banco* (A Scrip or deposit or subscription Receipt) represented no coin, and as little did it represent, as some have supposed, a superior value caused by the high credit of the bank.

Whatever the reason for the particular ratio selected, the establishment of a nominal *bank ducat* superior to the real ducat was an administrative provision probably made when the bank

---

[12] It is probably to a suspension during this war that Matthew Lewis refers, in his pamphlet A Large Model of a Bank (London, 1678), when he says that in the late Turkish wars the Senate was forced to expend the specie " now there is no money at all, neither is any money in specie ever paid out, but. ... the Fund is a mere imaginary thing."

[13] This, for example, is the statement made by Turbolo so early as 1629; by Malynes in 1656; by the writer of the Discorso printed in the Appendix, who wrote around 1760; and by Ricard and the other commercial writers near the end of the eighteenth century.

was opened or shortly after.[14] It was, in fact, simply the creation of a fictional currency, for use in accounting. The language of the *Discorso* as to what really took place when the bank was still in full operation leaves no doubt on the point. If, says the writer, a person carries 1,200 real ducats, *ducati effetivi*, to the bank, he receives credit for 1,000 ducats *banco*; and if, having credit for 1,000 *ducats banco*, he draws it out, and 1,200 real ducats are paid to him. The so-called constant *agio* of twenty percent was then simply the result of using two coinages to express the same real value.

The *agio* presumed freedom of deposit and freedom of withdrawal; and, such freedom being upheld, the *agio* would hardly rise and could not fall. It would not rise so long as *credit* in bank could be obtained by depositing coin, and it could not fall so long as 1,200 real ducats could be drawn for every 1,000 ducats banco. If there were a scarcity of bankable coin, the ducat *banco*, being required for certain payments, might conceivably be "cornered"; but this could not affect its relation to coin, and it could not depreciate except in the case of deferment. The 1,200 real ducats with which the depositor obtained his credit for 1,000 ducats *banco* were, however, ducats of lawful heft: whereas the coin in actual use in Venice, as in the other commercial cities of that age, consisted, to a great extent, of pieces below the

---

[14] Turbolo's statement, made in 1629, is that the difference of twenty percent. existed da molto tempo. Trevisan, writing near the close of the same century and after examination of the documents, says expressly, after describe ing the foundation of the bank, " In questo momento si stabili anche una mo neta propria per il medesimo banco," etc. Informazzone, p. 296. Malynes, Lex Mercatortia (edition of 1656), describes (p. 257) many cases of what he calls im aginary money. Among them is the Venetian ducat banco, but he does not re mark upon it as in any way unusual

standard, either from wear or from illegal practices, constituting a currency often much depreciated.

The coin of full weight then bore an adjustable premium when exchanged for that in usual circulation; and thus, we have what was called the *sur-agio*, which had to be taken into reducing bank money to every-day cash. [15] The agio represented the difference between the coinages used by the bank and by the public in dealing with standard money, and the *sur-agio* measured the depreciation of circulating coin below the legal standard.

These were the conditions under which the *Bancogiro* carried on its operations when receiving, transferring, and paying out, according to the structure of its charter. The implementation of this structure was several times disturbed, however, as we have seen, by deferment of payment. Considering the difficulty found even by the present generation in realizing such cases, it is not astounding that in the seventeenth century the Bank of Venice should have seemed to have in use a "*fiat currency*," free of any cash basis, and, yet, of higher credit than even coin itself. But the Venetian Senate was not always cautious as to the use of credits in bank, but, as in the case referred to above, yielded to the temptation or necessity of over-issue. The inevitable result then followed, - the ducat *banco* depreciated, anyhow its use in settlements for exchange and the supposed credit of the

---

[15] Thus Kruse, *Allgemeiner Contorist* (Hamburg, 1753), p. 174, says, "Die Valuta ist entweder Banco, oder Corrente, oder Piccoli," and then goes on to explain that Banco bears an agio of twenty percent in Corrente, and Corrente an agio of twenty-nine percent in *Piccoli*, defining the three valute substantially as above.

republic. The malevolent was of the simplest nature possible; and the remedy was as simple.

The *Bank of Venice* existed for more than six centuries, or until the subversion of the Republic in 1797. It became the parent of several other celebrated banking institutions, such as those of Barcelona, of Genoa—which, for a considerable time, held the island of Corsica in pledge—of Hamburg, and of Amsterdam.

(Above) The Campo di Rialto, c.1760. (Below) The Banco Del Giro in Rialto in 1320

Figure 2 First actual building and sign board of any Bank, 1619

Figure 3 The Market where once Banco Del Giro in Rialto was located.

*"Then have ye Lombard Street, so called of the Longobards and other merchants; strangers of diverse nations assembling there twice every day. Of what original, or continuance, I have not read of record, more than that Edward the Second, in the twelfth of his reign, confirmed a messuage, sometime belonging to Robert Turke, abutting on Lombard Street toward the south, and toward Cornhill on the north, for the merchants of Florence, which proveth the street to have had the name of Lombard Street before the reign of Edward the Second."*

Penned John Stow, in his *"Survey of the Cities of London and Westminster,"* in 1598. A public debt, contracted in the later-half of twelfth century, is said to have been made transferable like a modern registered debt, then to have been found useful as a medium of payment, to have become the nucleus of a system of deposits and transfers of money, and so to have developed into a bank of deposit of the primitive type, holding a place of great thought variable importance in European commerce for more than six centuries.

Lombard Street, in the Longbourn Ward of London,[16] was selected by the place of business by the earliest goldsmiths, money changers and money-lenders from the earliest times. It is unclear when these businesses, predominately conducted by the

---

[16] (Allen, 1839 p. 680) This ward according to Stow, 'is so called from a long borne (bourn) of sweet water, which in old times breaking out into Fenchurch street, ran down the same street and Lombard street, to the west of St. Mary Woolnoth's Church.

Jews, who emigrated to William the Conqueror, but subjected to miseries and social-ill treatments. A tale tells that in 1264, the interest rate was close to 50 percent in Lombard Street.[17]

The *"Longobards"* of Lombard Street were doubtless the original bankers in the Great Britain, though some sort of dealing in money as goods, consisting largely in the exchange of foreign and English coins, was carried on, long prior to their presence in the country, by the Jews. The Longobards combined the business of pawn-broking with money-exchange, gold and silversmithry.

The banking did not emerge into Lombard Street until the Medici family of Italy has established relations with the money-changers of Lombard Street, in London and the Lombards adopted the badge with three pillars of Medici family[18]. Recorded in London Directory of 1677, out of fifty-eight bankers in London, thirty-eight were located in Lombard Street. These bankers and merchants were wealthy and the city of London was full of noticeable residences belonging to them [19]. Some names of houses, and identification signs are listen here;

### FLOWER DE LUCE

Benjamin Hinton was first mentioned in 1663, and he kept a large account with Backwell, which was a sort of clearing account, before 1672. In 1702, he is described as deceased and bankrupt.

---

[17] (PRICE, 1887). 1264, the rate of interest was more than 40 per cent., for it is related that 500 Jews were slain by the citizens of London, because one of them would have forced a Christian to pay more than two-pence for the usury of twenty shillings for one week, which sum of two-pence they were allowed by the King to take from the Scholars of Oxford.

[18] (PRICE, 1887) The Medici Family in London.

[19] (PRICE, 1887) in 1677, the city was full of fine residences for merchants.

### ANGEL AND CROWN

John Ewing and Benjamin Norrington, goldsmiths and notes issuers, were there by 1677. Later in 1688, the house was occupied Henry Limbrey, and in 1698 by John and Thomas Cox.

### THE ROSE

Henry Nelthorpe, also Thomas Nelthorpe were occupants in 1677. In 1694, a goldsmith name Lane, who sold Copper Medals to Charles I, was occupant.

### THE THREE TUNNS

John Temple and John Seale were occupants, and they went bankrupt in 1678. The became an Inn in 1748 and then it was burnt down.

### THE MEARMAIN

A goldsmith Edward Delves was there from 1586-1638. In 1644, Hacker, a goldsmith was there. In 1677, it was the house of Peter Wade, a goldsmith.

There were 97 houses in Lombard street according to the "accurate map of the City of London" by John Ogilvy, but after the Great Fire in 1666, many of them were destroyed. In 1799, there were 74 left. There are rarely any records of the residents of Lombard streets, before 17th century, and after the Great Fire, many of the residents scattered. A few names, though, I can collect from the historic records.

The parable of the slothful servant, in which it is said, *"Thou oughtest to have put my money to the exchangers, and then at my coming I should have received mine own with usury,"* shows that the Jews, as a nation, well understood the art of speculation; but the system, in all prospect, was as rude as all oriental banking has persisted to the present moment.

**Tokens of Lombard Street Tradesmen**

Italian, basically Venetian bankers, after being stripped from Private banking in Venice, well accustomed with the skill of banking, as practiced in Venice, settled in London in sizable population towards the latter part of the sixteenth century, and, probably, got into early connection with the previously-established money-lenders—the goldsmiths and the Jews. The business was then very profitable, but also exceedingly dangerous, the lending of money not having yet been made legal—this only took place in 1546—and passing by the ugly name of usury. A mysterious and no less terrible incident in these banking transactions of former times is mentioned in Arnold's *"Chronicle."*

The old historian daintily records that in 1278 *"all the goldsmiths of London, with all those that kept the Change, and many other men of the City, were arrested and taken for buying of plates of silver, and for change of great money for small money, which were indicted by the wards of the City; and on the Monday next after the Epiphany, the justices sitting at the Guildhall to make deliverance, that is to say. Sir Stephen of Pencestre, Sir John of Cobham, and other with that these last [pleased] to associate to them, and there were prejudged and drawn and hanged three English Christian men, and two hundred four score and twelve English Jews."* It looks the shrewd Lombards escaped being "drawn and hanged" together with their Christian and Jewish brethren, which was due in all probability to the high favour which they enjoyed at Court and among the aristocracy.

Henry IV., borrowed very largely from the *"Longobards"*— by which term must be understood merchants of the four Republics of Genoa, Lucca, Florence, and Venice—so also did several of his forbearers and scions. It is stated in the eighth volume of the *"Foedera"* that in 1404 the "Society of the Genoese" advanced one thousand marks, and Medici Family of

Florence five hundred marks, to the Crown, with the understanding *"to pay themselves out of the customs which shall from time to time become due by their ships importing merchandize to London, Southampton, and Sandwich ; as also out of the duties on wool, leather, cloth, and other merchandize which the said ships shall export from the said three ports into foreign parts."* In the following year, the like sums were advanced to the King by the two Lombard societies, on the same security for repayment. It is curious that in none of those loans is there any mention of the word *interesse*, nor of any term denoting usury or interest on money. There is little doubt, however, that the Lombard bankers were well paid some way or other; they, at any rate, enjoyed a desirable immunity from being drawn and hanged like ordinary "English Christian men."

During the whole of the middle ages the trade in money was mainly in the hands of a number of persons called the *Royal Exchangers*. There were severe laws against exporting English coin; and the exchanging of the money of the realm for foreign coin or bullion was held to be an especial Royal distinction, a *"flower of the Crown."* An important official, the King's Exchanger, was alone entitled to pass the current coins of the realm to merchant strangers for those of their respective countries, and to supply foreign money to those who were going abroad, whether aliens or natives.

The house in which this business was transacted was commonly called the Exchange. In the reign of King John, the place of the Exchange in London was in the street now called the Old Change Court, near St. Paul's. In the reign of Henry VII., the office of "*Royal Exchanger*" fell into disuse; but it was re-established in 1627 by Charles *I*, who asserted in a proclamation on the subject that no person of whatever quality, trade, or profession, had a right to meddle with the exchange of moneys without a special license from the Crown. At the same time the King appointed the Earl of Holland to the sole office of "*Changer,*

Exchanger, and Outchanger," which appointment gave rise to a vast amount of dissatisfaction, particularly in the city of London. Thereupon a pamphlet was published the next year by the King's authority—"*Cambium Regius, or the Office of His Majesty's Exchanger Royal*"— defending the King's prerogative, which, it was stated, had been exercised without dispute from the time of Henry I., until the reign of Henry VIII., when it ceased on account of the coin becoming so debased that no exchange could be made. A further reason was given in the fact that *"for above thirty years past it has been the usual practice of those exchanging goldsmiths to make their servants run every morning from shop to shop to buy up all weighty coins for the mints of Holland and the East Countries, whereby the King's mint had stood still."*

The steady progress of the occupation of "*goldsmitherie*" into the banking business is here specified. It is still further outlined in a rare pamphlet of the date of 1676, entitled *"The Mystery of the New-fashioned Goldsmiths, or Bankers, Discovered."* The pamphlet says that the London merchants were generally habituated to deposit their money in the Tower, in the care of the Master of the Mint. Charles took advantage of this circumstance by nabbing, shortly before the meeting of the Long Parliament, £200,000, professedly as a loan, but not only without the approval, but to the extreme resentment of the luckless owners. Of course, no more money after that time found its way into the Mint.

Not knowing where to hide their cash, in the dreadful uncertainty of the times, the traders then, according to the pamphlet, entrusted their assets, distributed in small portions, to their clerks and apprentices, and the latter, not unfrequently, were unable to resist the enticement of taking to themselves the contents of their pockets. Consequently, a new and safer mode of giving money in trust became necessary. First time about 1640, businesses, and individuals began placing their funds in the hands of the goldsmiths, who formed a company by permission of Edward IV.

Accepting the trust of the merchants, the goldsmiths incorporated the business of buying and selling plate, foreign and English coins from the money entrusted to them. The wealth and reputation of the corporation at once gave confidence in the new mode of investment, and made it spread very rapidly. *"Much about the same time,"* the pamphlet continues, *"the goldsmiths began to receive the rents of gentlemen's estates remitted to town, and to allow them and others who put cash into their hands some interest for it. This was a great allurement for people to put their money into their hands, which would bear interest till the day they wanted it."* The goldsmiths usually gave receipts for the money in notes, which, passing from hand to hand, became a virtual kind of bank notes. So, profitable was this business that some of the most enterprising goldsmiths soon gave up their original trade, and became solely bankers. Among the first who did so was *Francis Child*[20]. Pennant calls him *"the father of the profession."*

---

[20] http://heritagearchives.rbs.com/people/list/francis-child-i.html

Signs in Lombard Street, London,
the birth place of Banking in England

Lombard Street, the Birthplace of British Banking Today

CORNHILL, AND LOMBARD STREET, FROM THE POULTRY.

# THE *BANK OF ENGLAND*

The stability and conventional character of trade and commerce of British metropolis, is singularly illustrated by the fact that there should now be in London many businesses continued in the same family, and often, too, in the same house, for two or three centuries. Such an example is the banking-house of *Child and Co.,* near Temple Bar. *Francis Child,* the *"father of the profession,"* founded the banking business in the old house in Fleet Street, at the accession of Charles II.; but even earlier, banking, combined with *"goldsmitherie,"* was carried on at the same place, probably for a century and more, by a worthy and wealthy race of citizens, called *"Wheeler"*[21].

The last male descendant of the line, William Wheeler, died in 1663, having previously given his only daughter, Elizabeth, in marriage to his dependable novice, Francis Child. The latter, a man of great energy, wisdom, and foresight, was not long to perceive that the business of banking was far more important, as well as more lucrative, than the occupation of goldsmith, which his father-in-law had carried on as principal business. In consequence, Francis Child threw off the limitations of the trade, and thus became *the first English banker*. Others followed in his steps, founding many other institutions.

The origin of *Hoare's bank*, in Fleet Street, is traced back to 1680, and that of *Snow's*, in the Strand, to 1685. The firm of *Stone, Martin, and Stone*, of Lombard Street, claim to be the immediate successors of *Sir Thomas Gresham*, the "royal merchant," the celebrated founder of the Exchange. Francis Child, after a prosperous career, died on the 4th of October,

---

[21] The Term "Wheeler-Dealer" originated from "Wheeler".

1713, full of age and honours, leaving his business to his two sons, James and William. Francis Child became Sheriff of London in 1691, Lord Mayor in 1699, and M.P. for the city in the first of Queen Anne, 1702. The honours of knighthood were the last that fell upon the "father of the profession," who died as Sir Francis Child.

Nothing occurred to mar the quiet progress of the practice of banking till 1694, when the establishment of the *Bank of England* gave an enormous increase to the business. The founder of the *Bank of England,* William Paterson, was a very remarkable man. Of the early history of William Paterson, very little that can be called authentic is known. According to some accounts he studied theology, became subsequently a missionary in the West Indies, and finally a buccaneer in the same regions. All this, however, is tolerably apocryphal.

What seems more certain is, that William Paterson was born in the parish of Tynwald the county of Dumfriesshire, Scotland, about 1660; that he was of respectable if not wealthy parents, and that he more than once sat for Dumfriesshire, in the parliament of Scotland. A great desire for travelling drove him abroad at an early age, and he spent some six or seven years of his life in visiting nearly all the countries of Europe, besides the West Indies and part of the continent of America.

There are stories about his having lost his paternal opulence, as outlawed Presbyterian, and of his wandering about as a peddler for some part of this period through London and the neighbouring countries; but all this is again mere rumour, founded on no authenticated facts. That the travelling experience had something to do with his elaborate schemes and concepts regarding banking and money-dealings, seems highly probable, for at the period when William Paterson visited the chief countries of the Continent, there were no less than eight public banking establishments in operation, all in a more or less flourishing state. They were[22]:—

| Name of Bank | Year of Foundation |
| --- | --- |
| Bank of Venice | 1157 |
| Bank of Geneva | 1345 |
| Bank of Barcelona | 1401 |
| Bank of Genoa | 1407 |
| Bank of Amsterdam | 1607 |
| Bank of Hamburg | 1619 |
| Bank of Rotterdam | 1635 |
| Bank of Stockholm | 1688 |

---

[22]  Dictionary of dates, and universal reference by Joseph Timothy Haydn, 1841

Paterson seems to have laid his first projects connected with banking before the traders of Rotterdam and Amsterdam, who, however, turned a deaf ear to them, wary as ever of foreign advice, particularly English.

He came back to England, where he found unexpected support. In seeking to establish a national bank, on the model of that of Venice and others, William Paterson pursued what had been the great object of English statesmen and traders. This entity was very seriously discussed during the civil wars and under the Commonwealth. The countenance shown by Cromwell to the Jews favoured it, and at the early sittings of the first Council of Trade at Mercers' Hall, after the Restoration, a proposition was brought forward for *"the establishment of Banks and Lombards among us, as in Holland."*

Various writers treated the matter, and the favour which the plan found among the traders of London, was no doubt increased by the arbitrary shutting-up of the Exchequer under Charles II. It was at such a propitious time that William Paterson came forward with a very complete plan for a national bank, which, as it was the work of a mind thoroughly aware with the business, was received with nearly widespread admiration. His proposal was straightaway accepted, the basis of the *"new Bank of England"* being a loan of £1,200,000 for the public service.

The *Bank of England* thus had exactly the same origin as the banks of Venice, the oldest in Europe. What brought the English Government so readily to accept Paterson's plan was its need of money, due partly to frequent blemishes and misuses in the system of taxation, and partly to the supposed uncertainty of the new revolutionary rule. King William himself was greatly in favour of the undertaking, and hastened the grant of a license of incorporation to the bank, dated July 27, 1694.

The charter declared, amongst other things, that *"the governor and company of the Bank of England"* should be capable, in law, *"to purchase, enjoy, and retain, to them and their successors, any monies, lands, rents, tenements, and possessions whatsoever, and to purchase and acquire all sorts of goods and chattels whatsoever."* It was settled likewise, that *"the management and government of the corporation be committed to the governor and twenty-four directors, who shall be elected between the 25th day of March and the 25th day of April each year, from among the members of the company, duly qualified."* The qualifications were that *"they must be natural-born subjects of England, or naturalized subjects, who shall have in their own name, and for their own use, severally, viz. the governor at least £4,000 the deputy-governor £3,000, and each director £2,ooo."*

The money required was subscribed in less than ten days. In return for the loan of £1,200,000, Government guaranteed an annual payment of £100,000 to the *Bank of England,* namely, eight percent, interest on the amount advanced, and £4,000 a year for expenses of management. Great, accordingly, was the eagerness of affluent men to invest their cash in so gainful an enterprise. In a curious letter written by one, Mr. Locke to a friend at Amsterdam, during the ten days that the subscription lists were lying open, it is said: — *"Your friend J. F. (John Furley) has taken £300 to the new bank which has already got a capital of £1,000,000. I shall myself subscribe for £ 500 at once, and it will be full to-night."* The rush for investments, it seems, took place in the last ten days, the fire of patriotism and the desire after the eight percent interest, having been stimulated by a concerned movement of several private bankers towards the *Bank of England.*

William Paterson hardly gained the benefit of the great idea which he had realized in so short a time. He was one of the first directors of the bank, upon a stipulation of £2,000 stock, which, however, he sold out before the end of a year, in 1695, and thus willingly removed from the board. What brought him to take this step is not clearly known; but it is generally avowed that more wealthy men than himself took advantage of his abilities, and then tricked him of the reward. But there is scarcely more proof for this assertion than the statement of Sir John Dalrymple, who says: — *"The persons to whom he applied made use of his ideas, took the honour to themselves; were civil to him awhile, and neglected him afterwards."* Another writer pretends: *"The friendless Scot was intrigued out of his post and out of the honours he had earned."* Probably Mr. Francis, the historian of the *Bank of England,* is not far from the truth when he says: *"The name of William Paterson was not long upon the list of directors. The facts which led to his departure from the honourable post of director are difficult to collect; but it is not at all improbable that the character of Paterson was too speculative for those with whom he was joined in companionship."*

The enduring part of William Paterson's history is very sad, and involved, like his previous career, in much mystery. Having retired from the management of the *Bank of England,* he progressed to carry out the other objectives of his life, which was to found "a free commonwealth in Darien." He succeeded so far as to form a company of trading entrepreneurs, under the title of **"The Company of Scotland trading to Africa and the Indies."** The main purpose of the company was to establish a British colony stretching over the whole Isthmus of Panama, which colony, Paterson believed, would become a leading station on the highway of the world, forming the emporium where the trade of the East would meet that of the West. The plan was by no means impracticable, and had it been fully carried out, according to the intentions of the projector, might have had infinite significances for trade and civilization. However, it did not succeed, owing mostly to disagreements among the leaders of the enterprise, and to the concealed opposition of the English Government.

On the 26th of July, 1698, *"twelve hundred men sailed in five stout ships"* on the ill-fated Darien expedition, from the harbour of Leith; but Paterson had no share in the conduct of the enterprise, and boarded with the fleet as private adventurer. What with the gross mismanagement of the council of seven, the opposition of the home Government, and other unfavourable circumstances, the colonial project proved utter collapse.

Though tumble-down by the catastrophe of his dearest hopes, he condemned nobody, but continued to struggle on in the development of new schemes and plans for extending British trade and commerce. He had an important share in the union of the English and Scottish Parliaments, and was incessant in his endeavours to relieve the distress of his native country. At the treaty of union, a guarantee in favour of Paterson was recommended to Queen Anne by the Scottish Parliament, on the ground of his "carrying on matters of a public nature, much to his country's service." But George I ascended the throne before the indemnity was paid.

The remainder of his years, till his death, in January, 1719, Paterson spent in London, in unavailing hostility to the ruinous schemes of his relative and old financial foe, John Law. Considering the greatness of the work he achieved, a statue of William Paterson would, not be out of place in the central hall of the *Bank of England.*

The bank of England - nicknamed the Old Lady - has been on its current site in the City of London since 1734. Photo / BANK OF ENGLAND ARCHIVE

The old Mercer's Hall, where the Bank of England was first established

SEALING OF THE BANK OF ENGLAND CHARTER. 1694.
SIR JOHN HOUBLON,
Governor.
SIR JOHN SOMERS.
Lord Keeper.
MR. MICHAEL GODFREY
Deputy Governor.

Bank of England 5/- dollar

# THE MONEYED INTEREST

The institution of the *Bank of England* gave rise to the growth of a power hitherto unknown in the country, the *"moneyed interest."* The term never occurred in the common use till the latter part of the seventeenth century, when, about 1692, it was first used by some pamphleteers as a title of derision. "The centre of jobbing," says one of these writers, who discusses the "moneyed interest" from his own point of view, clearly the moneyless one: *"the centre of jobbing is in the kingdom of Change Alley and its adjacencies. The limits are easily surrounded in about a minute and a half. Stepping out of Jonathan's into the Alley, you turn your face full south; moving on a few paces, and then turning due east, you advance to Garraway's; from thence, going out at the other door, you go on still east into Birchin Lane; and then, halting a little at the Sword-Blade Bank, you immediately face to the north, enter Comhill, visit two or three petty provinces there on your way to the west; and thus, having boxed your compass, and sailed round the stock-jobbing globe, you turn into Jonathan's again."*

The pamphleteers, looking down from their Grub Street garrets into this world of cash and of scrip, turned pale for envy and anger, and tried, as best they could, to insult the nouveaux treasures. Among these envied parvenus was *Sir Robert Clayton,* director of the *Bank of England,* whose villa was the boast of the Surrey hills, whose banqueting rooms were wainscoted with cedar; whose entertainments imitated those of kings; and whose judicious benevolence made him the pride of the City, and procured him a seat in the House of Commons.

Another of the number was *Sir Henry Furnese,* likewise a director of the *Bank of England,* and one of the most enterprising men of the day. He maintained, at his private expense, a complete and perfect train of intelligence through Holland,

Flanders, France, and Germany. In not a few instances, he received the news of important events such as battles, long before the Government; and the fall of Namur, among others, largely added to his profits, owing to his early intelligence. At times, he condescended to communicate such intelligence to His Majesty's Ministers, which loyalty King William rewarded on more than one occasion by costly presents. The pamphleteers reproach Sir Henry Furnese with having fabricated news, and having turned his *"Reuter"* agency to the most mercenary account.

It is said that if Sir Henry wished to buy, his brokers were ordered to look gloomy and mysterious, hint at important news, and even effect bogus sales. Their movements, of course, were closely watched; the pollution spread; and the speculators having got fairly alarmed, the prices lowered not unfrequently 4 or 5 percent. Then it was the time for other, agents to buy—of course to the enormous profit of their employer. Similar stories are told of the wealthy Jew banker, *Sir Solomon de Medina*, who accompanied Marlborough in all his campaigns. It is tolerably well proven that he prevailed upon the avarice of the great commander to accept a regular annuity of six thousand pounds. He largely repaid himself by expresses containing early intelligence of the great battles fought; and Ramilies, Oudenarde, and Blenheim, directed as much to the purse of the shrewd Hebrew banker as they did to the glory of the English nation.

In reply to the numerous attacks, mostly of anonymous writers, upon the *Bank of England* and the "moneyed interest," a notable little pamphlet, rather important in the history of banking, was published about 1694, by *Michael Godfrey*, the deputy-governor of the Bank. The pamphlet, afterwards reprinted in the Somers Collection, bears the title *"A Short Account of the Bank of England,"* and consists of nearly twelve pages' quarto. Godfrey's object is to prove *"that the Bank, notwithstanding all the Cavils, which the Wit and Malice of its opponents have raised, is one of the best establishments that ever was made for the Good of the Kingdom."* In attempting to prove his claim, the author enters into many interesting details regarding bankers and banking.

He notices, as a peculiar advantage of the Bank of England , "the Ease and Security of the great Receipts and Payments of Money which are made by the Bank, where People's Cash is kept as it is at the Goldsmith's;" and he thinks it worthwhile to remind his readers "how much Money has been lost in England by the Goldsmiths and Scriveners Breaking, which in about 30 years past, cannot amount to so little as betwixt Two and Three Millions, all which might have been prevented had a Bank been sooner Established."

And the author contends further that "the Bank being thus useful to the Public, extends itself likewise to accommodate all Private Men's Occasions; for they lend Money on Mortgages and real Securities at 5 percent, per annum, and their very Publishing they would do it has given a Check to the raising the Interest on them from 5 to 6 percent, per annum as was attempted; and if the Titles of Land were made more secure, Money would be Lent thereon at 4 percent, per annum, and in time of Peace at 3 percent, per annum. Foreign Bills of Exchange are discounted at 4 percent, per annum, and Inland Bills and Notes for Debts at 6 percent, per annum, and those who keep their Cash in the Bank have the one discounted at 3 percent, per annum, for which most Goldsmiths used to take 9 or 10 percent, per annum. And Money is lent on Pawns of Commodities which are not perishable, at 5 percent, per annum, for which some, in their Necessities, have paid more than double as much, to the Ruin of many great Traders."

But the greatest benefit which, in the author's opinion, the Bank of England has conferred upon the public, and is going to confer, is that "the Bank, besides the raising; £1,200,000 towards the Chaise of the War, cheaper than it could otherwise have been done, and, like the other Public Funds tying the People faster to the Government will infallibly lower the Interest of Money, as well on Public as Private Securities. And the lowering of Interest, besides the encouragement it will be to Industry, and Improvements, will by a natural consequence raise the Value of Land." The foregoing paragraph is noticeable in more than one respect.

In this "tying the People faster to the Government," Mr. Godfrey touched the very point on which, willingly or covertly, most of the furious pamphleteers attacked the *Bank of England*. The Bank was a Whig project, and had been eminently successful in supporting the leaders of the party in the prosecution of the war. This, as it had excited the warmest feelings of joy and congratulation among the friends of the party, had also created bitter rage and indignation among their political enemies. In the end, seeing their impotency otherwise to hurt the great financial structure, the Tories determined to get up a rival establishment, on a much larger scale than the *Bank of England*. The capital was to be £2,564,000, advanced in loans on the same principle as that of the *Bank of England*; but with this proviso, that the trading capital and notes were to be advanced solely to landowners, for the cultivation of land, and at the rate of 3 percent.

The scheme, brought forward under the title of the "*Land Bank*," was due to Dr. Hugh Chamberlain, and, being warmly patronized by the Tory party, received the sanction of Parliament in April, 1696. The time for taking subscriptions was limited, in the like manner as had been done in the case of the *Bank of England*. When the subscriptions opened, the Lords of the Treasury put down £5,000 on behalf of the government; but this was nearly all the support received, for the whole of the subscriptions on the part of the public amounted only to £2,100. Consequently, the *Land Bank* proved a total and complete failure. It was a time of great financial depression; but though the *Bank* of *England* suffered under the general disorder, it successfully weathered the storm, after a short and partial suspension of cash payments.

In his defence of the *Bank of England*, Michael Godfrey has some interesting remarks, which throw considerable light upon the earlier practice of banking. *"It is alleged by some,"* he *says, "that the Bank will engross all manner of trades; but this is an objection, like many others which are made against it, by those who do not understand its constitution. The Goldsmiths have been guilty of Engrossing most commodities themselves, and they have also been great Merchants and Traders. Since the nation has suffered so much by their Monopolizing Goods, and Trading with Other Men's stocks, it may seem highly Reasonable that as the Bank is restrained from Trade, for fear of those Mischiefs which the Goldsmiths have practiced, so the Goldsmiths, in like manner, should be limited to the Selling Plate and Jewels, which was their ancient and proper Trade. And if there be an Advantage to be made by the Running Cash of the Kingdom, it's fitter for the Bank to have it, which consists of 1,300 persons, and who employ it to serve the Nation in general, by lowering the Interest of Money, than that it should be given to a few private Men."*

Here is the earliest argument in favour of joint-stock banks over private banks. The joint-stock bankers of those days knew how to do full justice to the recommendation of the "advantage to be made by the Running Cash of the Kingdom." Michael Godfrey, the able champion of the Bank, died a heroic death, strangely illustrative of the career of bank directors of the olden time. As deputy-governor of the *Bank of England*, he came into repeated contact with King William, his ministers, and generals, and not unfrequently had to follow them to the wars. At the time the King undertook the siege of Namur, in July, 1695, there were some important negotiations pending between the Bank and the Government, and, to expedite them, Godfrey went over to the Netherlands.

Arrived at Namur, he was admitted into the intimacy of King William, with whom he had frequent conversations regarding the supply of money—then, as now, well known to be the "sinews of war." Conversing thus one day, during a heavy cannonade, both banker and King ventured too near the enemy, and a heavy shot struck down the deputy-governor of the *Bank of England* at the side of his Majesty.

It was the first time in history— and will, probably, be the last—of a banker killed by a cannon ball in the exercise of his duties.

# THE SOUTH SEA BUBBLE

One of the more immediate consequences of the successful creation of the *Bank of England* was the rise of a number of effervesce companies, professedly engaged in banking, but in reality, in cheating the public out of their money. The pioneer of these fictitious undertakings was a company called the *"Mine Adventurers of England,"* at the head of whom was *Sir Humphrey Mackworth*, who turned out to be one of the cleverest scoundrels of the time.

The *"Mine Adventurers"* had made banking their principal business, and their issue of notes in a short time became so large as seriously to alarm the Government and the directors of the *Bank of England*. To put a stop to the issue of notes— which was considered at the time an essential feature in banking; so, essential, in fact, as to constitute the very foundation of the business— it was enacted by Parliament *"that during the continuance of the corporation of the Governor and Company of the Bank of England, it shall not be lawful for any body politic or corporate whatsoever to borrow, owe, or take up any sum or sums of money in their bills or notes payable at demand."* The same clause prohibited the creation of any bank with more than six partners: that law was enacted particularly as a protection for the *Bank of England*. It was so understood at the time, and it did indeed have the effect of preventing any other joint-stock bank from being formed for some time after. It did not prevent, however, the growth of colossal bubbles that ever appeared in the financial world of the time. The crown and climax of these swindling concerns was the famous *South Sea Company*.

The scheme was projected by *Sir John Blunt*, a shrewd speculator in the capitals. He was accustomed to preach against the corruption and luxury of the age, and to insist upon high moral rectitude and puritanical severity of manners. Pope has immortalised his "tearless eyes": —

*"God cannot love,' says Blunt, with*
*tearless eyes;*

*The wretch he starves, and piously*
*denies."*

The charmingly simple object of Blunt's scheme was to emancipate the national debt, by reducing all the funds into one. On the 22nd of January, 1720, the House of Commons resolved itself into a committee to take the plan into consideration; and a subsequent proposition made by the South Sea Company, to unite the whole of the debts of the State, amounting to £30,981,712 at 5 percent until 1727, and after that period at 4 percent—for which they were to pay three million and a half—met with great admiration from most of the members of the House as well as the Government.

The friends of the *Bank of England* in Parliament gained, with great difficulty, a deferment of the question for five days, which delay was made use of by the Bank authorities, who offered in the meanwhile five million for the same rights, being an advance of one million and a half on the proposal of the *South Sea Company*. The latter thus bid seven and a half millions, on which rate again the *Bank of England* advanced, by offering to issue £1,700 Bank Stock for every hundred pounds absolute long annuities.

Fortunately for the *Bank of England*, but unfortunately for the country, the offer of the South Sea Company met with extreme popularity. The former ceased its bidding, and the latter remained in possession of its toxic bargain. At one time, there appears to have been some idea of dividing the *"advantages"* between the Bank and the South Sea Company; but Sir John Blunt on being consulted at once negatived this proposition by exclaiming, *"No, sir, we will never divide the child."*

The story of the rise and fall of the South Sea Company— the one of the most gigantic financial nuisance the world of the time has ever seen—need not be repeated here. The directors were dealers while the success of the swindle lasted, and boldly administered to the cupidity of their disciples. Dukes and duchesses had their hundreds of thousands, and secretaries of state their tens of thousands. Everybody speculated, and everybody rejoiced —while it lasted. For a time, companies of all kinds were started; prices of the most extravagant description were realized, and notions of the most extraordinary character brought forward. Two persons, a lady and a gentleman, declined to realize less than £3,000,000 each, at which price the latter thought he might purchase the crown of Poland.

The effervesce rose to its highest point in June, 1720, when South Sea stock was sold at above £1,000. All possible artifices were resorted to for maintaining this monstrous price. The representatives of the directors— "some of whom, by this time, had been created baronets, *"for their great services"*— threw out enigmatic hints about mines of hidden treasure newly discovered in the "South Seas;" while vessels filled to the brim with gold and diamonds were freely spoken of as about to release their treasures at London Bridge.

For a while the public mind seemed to be completely overwhelmed, so that nearly all the available resources of the kingdom were embarked in the wildest of speculations. Change Alley was swarming from morn to night with peers of the kingdom, country gentlemen, high-born ladies, and even dignitaries of the Church, all eager to worship the golden calf. The King himself is believed to have embarked in speculations; so much is certain, that his Majesty's ugly Hanoverian mistresses—both the fat and the lean lady immortalised by Thackeray—made large fortunes, and, with considerable wisdom, invested their gains in the sandy soil of the Fatherland. *"I am tired of politics,"* writes Prior in the summer of 1720; *"I am tired of politics, and lost in the South Sea. The roaring of the waves and the madness of the people are justly put together. It is all wilder than St. Anthony's dream."*

In the autumn of 1720 the bubble ruptured at last, and people awoke from their dream. Public credit sustained a tremendous shock, and a large number of bankers and goldsmiths who had lent money on the security of the South Sea stock, were forced to stop payment. But few people succeeded in saving anything from the general shipwreck.

*Samuel Chandler*, the eminent Nonconformist divine, risked his whole fortune in the bubble, and, having lost it, was obliged to serve in a bookseller's shop while he continued his ministerial duties. The elder Scraggs made Gay a present of £1,000 stock, and, as the poet had been a previous purchaser, his gain at one time amounted to £20,000. He consulted Dr. Arbuthnot, who strongly advised him to sell out. The bard doubted, hesitated, and lost all. The doctor who gave such shrewd advice was too irresolute to act on his own opinion, and lost £2,000 but, with enviable philosophy, comforted himself by saying it would be only 2,000 more stairs to ascend.

In the first great cry of distress, produced by the ruin of so many people, the *Bank of England* endeavored to come to the rescue of the South Sea Company. At the instance of Sir Robert Walpole, a meeting was held, at which the Governor and directors were empowered to agree with the South Sea Company to circulate their bonds, in hopes of sustaining the credit of the country. A memorandum was hastily drawn up, by which the

*Bank of England* undertook to circulate £3,500,000 at 400 percent. Fortunately for the Bank, this memorandum was not legally ratified. The fall of many banking establishments produced an immediate run upon the *Bank of England*, compelling the directors to renounce the agreement. Legal proceedings were commenced by some of the South Sea shareholders, but not continued, owing to the dread of publicity and the impossibility to *"go into court with clean hands."*

However, public uproar compelled the House of Commons to take up the matter, and an undisclosed committee was appointed to inquire into the businesses of the South Sea Company. Subsequently, the governors, directors, and officers of the company were brought before the bar of the Commons, and although, probably, nearly the whole of the members were involved in the speculation, they renounced as a body that which they had done as individuals; asserting that the transactions had been corrupt, infamous, and dangerous. The proceedings in both Houses of Parliament, nevertheless, were very stormy. Some members were expelled, some ran away, and some were mulcted in heavy fines. Once more the *Bank of England* was called upon to assist the State in its difficulties, and to make good by "honest trading" the trouble that had been done by fictitious and fraudulent speculation.

While the South Sea bubble ruined thousands, it also made the fortune of a few shrewd investors. One of the most notable of these was *Thomas Guy*, the founder of *Guy's Hospital*, whose chequered life forms a real essence of the period in which he lived. The son of a poor lighterman and coal dealer at Horselydown, Thomas Guy was put as a novice to a bookseller in 1660, and subsequently set up in craft by himself, in a very small way, at a shop forming the angle between Cornhill and Lombard Street. He made some money here in selling Bibles, and trebled the capital thus acquired by dealing in scrip.

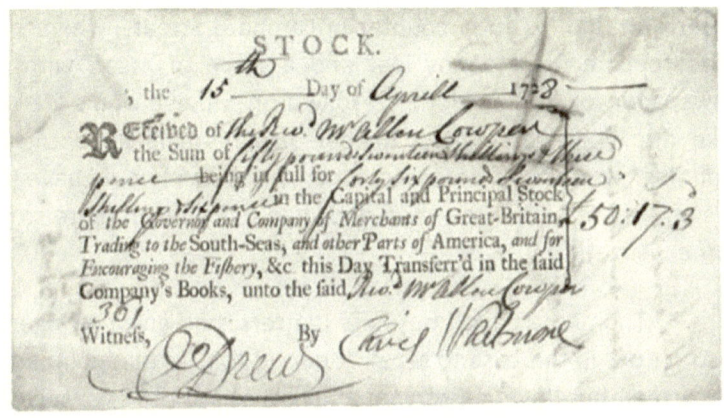

**SOUTH SEA COMPANY STOCK PHOTOS**

Always cool-headed and close-fisted, he was the very man to profit by the South Sea fever. When the tide was gradually rising, he at once began to see to what a deluge it would lead, and, slowly and carefully purchasing as much paper as he could lay hold of, he kept it till the paroxysm was at its height, and then, calculating that the waves could not possibly run any-further, even in times of general cascade and madness, he sold off the whole of his investments. In this way, he made nearly half a million pounds.

The half-million gained in the general wreck of the South Sea bubble went to charitable purposes through a very singular accident. Thomas Guy, grown very grey and very mean and miserly behind his shop counter in Lombard Street—where he used to dine on a penny loaf and a piece of meat, with a newspaper for a table-cloth—resolved on the eve of his life to take unto himself a partner in the person of his maid-servant. The weddings were being prepared, when, as chance would have it, the pavement before the shop door had to be taken up to stop some unsightly gaps.

Thomas, as in all business matters, had given stringent instructions in this case to repair the road to a certain point and no further; but the maid-servant, fully conscious of her expected elevation in the world, presumed upon revoking these orders, telling the paviors to improve the appearance of another bit of road a few inches beyond the appointed boundary. The whole matter involved only a few shillings, at the utmost.

However, *Thomas Guy* was so enraged by being put to an unnecessary expense, that he broke off the match with the too hasty kitchen lass, and, to spite her, committed to give the whole of his wealth for the foundation of a hospital. Thus, arose that glorious charity, on the Surrey side of London Bridge, still known as *Guy's Hospital*. The cost of founding this vast pile amounted to about £20,000; and he left an additional £220,000 as a grant. The founder likewise setup almshouses at Tamworth, in Staffordshire, his mother's birthplace, a borough which had paid honour to his golden guineas by electing him to a seat among the representatives of the nation.

Thomas Guy died in December, 1724, in the eighty-first year of his age, after having dedicated to charitable purposes more money than any other man in his time. It appears a singular relation of cause and consequence that the most gigantic swindling speculation of the eighteenth century gave rise to the most munificently endowed hospital in Great Britain.

**Thomas Guy**

# PRIVATE BANKERS

There is much of the romance of history in the origin of some of the great private banking houses—though all more or less threatened with destruction by the giant of joint-stock enterprise. The origin, among others, of the house of *Jones, Loyd, and Co.,* was very curious. *Lewis Loyd*, the founder of the house, father of the Lord Overstone, began his career as a Welsh dissenting minister in a small chapel at Manchester, the congregation of which included a Mr. Jones, a sort of half-banker, half-manufacturer.

In addition to Jones, there was a young Miss Jones who attended the sermons of the Rev. Mr. Loyd; and, as often happens, the maiden found the orations so eloquent that she fell in love with the preacher. The affection was responded to by the minister, and the couple, dreading the purse-proud trader would never permit the *mésalliance*. Of course, when the affair became known to Mr. Jones, he was furious; but, seeing that things went on pretty comfortably with his daughter, he became acquiescent in the end to his reverend son-in-law.

However, though fond of attending sermons, he did not think preaching a good business, and therefore proposed that Loyd should give up the Welsh dissenting chapel and enter his counting-house as a partner, under the firm of *Jones, Loyd, and Co.,* Loyd consented; and, to extend the business, it was subsequently agreed that he should go to London, and establish a bank under the name of the Manchester firm.

Henceforth, *Jones, Loyd, and Co., of Manchester*, drew bills upon *Jones, Loyd, and Co., of London*, or, as it was facetiously called at the time, *"pig upon bacon."* It soon turned out that Lewis Loyd was eminently fitted to be a banker; for his clearness of head, tireless diligence, and shrewdness proved the foundation of success for the new institution. After a very long and honourable career, Loyd retired from business, being succeeded as head of the London firm by his son, *Samuel Jones Loyd*, who was subsequently created *Lord Overstone*. Thus, the falling in love of a young Manchester girl with a Welsh dissenting minister was the foundation of the creation of an important bank, besides leading to the creation of a new peer of the realm.

The banking-house of *Coutts & Co.,* arose under circumstances not less striking than those connected with the history of Jones, Loyd, and Co. The father of Mr. Coutts was a trader at Edinburgh who had four sons, the two youngest of whom, James and Thomas, were brought up in the paternal counting-house. James, at the age of twenty-five, came to London, and first settled in St. Mary Axe as a Scotch merchant, from which business, however, he later retired to become a banker. He took a house in the Strand, and he was joined here, some years after, by his brother Thomas as a partner—the business being carried on under the name of *James and Thomas Coutts*. James Coutts died early, and Thomas was then left sole proprietor of the bank. His veracity soon gained him many friends, and made him remarkably successful in his business. A characteristic instance, both of his shrewdness and enterprise, is given by Lawson, in his *"History of Banking."*

In the early part of his career, Coutts, anxious to secure the cordial co-operation of the heads of the various banking houses in London, was in the routine of frequently pleasing them to dinner. On one of these occasions, the manager of a City bank accidentally remarked that a certain nobleman had applied to his firm for the loan of £30,000, and had been refused. Coutts listened, and said nothing; but the moment his guests had departed from the dinner, about ten o'clock in the evening, he reached the house of the nobleman mentioned, and requested an appointment for meeting next day.

On the following morning, the nobleman called at the bank. Coutts received him with the greatest respect, and taking thirty-one-thousand pound notes from a drawer, presented them to his lordship. The latter, very agreeably surprised, exclaimed: "But what security am I to give you."—"I shall be satisfied with your lordship's note of hand," was the reply. The I O U was instantly given, with the remark, "I find I shall only require for the present £10,000; I therefore return you £20,000, with which you will be pleased to open an account in my name." The generous—or, as it may more truly be called, exceedingly well-calculated—act of Coutts was not lost upon the nobleman, who, in addition to paying-in within a few months £200,000 to his account, the proceeds from the sale of an estate, recommended several high dignitaries to utilize the bank in the Strand. Among the new clients who did so utilize, it was King George III.

Coutts had not only many friends, but even real admirers among the nobility, and was an object of attraction to not a few designing matrons, who would have been but too happy to marry some noble but portionless daughter to the rich banker. These aristocratic matrimonial speculations were somewhat rudely dispelled by the choice which Coutts made of a wife, in the person of Elizabeth Starkey, a native in his brother's service. The union was productive, it is said, of great happiness to the banker; and, though children of a servant, his three daughters all married noblemen—namely, the *Marquis of Bute*, the *Earl of Guildford*, and *Sir Francis Burdett*.

After the death of his first wife, Coutts gave his hand to Mellon, an actress. On this second marriage, both Mr, and Mrs. Coutts were made the constant subjects of ridicule, which, however, had no other effect than that of strengthening the confidence of the husband in his wife. This confidence was displayed in a remarkable manner in the will made by Coutts before his death. By this will he left the whole of his fortune, amounting to above £900,000, to his widow, for her sole use and benefit, and at her absolute disposal, without the deduction of a single legacy to any other person.

Mrs. Coutts subsequently married the Duke of St. Albans; but under her marriage settlement wisely reserved to herself the whole control of the immense fortune left to her by her first husband. On her death, she bequeathed the vast property to the favorite grand-daughter of Coutts, Miss Angela Burdett—the estimable and beneficent lady, founder of so many churches and schools, who is well known as Miss Angela Burdett Coutts. Miss A. B. Coutts continues to be the principal proprietor of the old bank in the Strand; the business being conducted for her by trustees, under the old style of Coutts and Co.

The banking-house of Barclay and Co. sprang into existence about the same time as that of Coutts, and there are some interesting anecdotes connected with the history of its origin. One of these, somewhat apocryphal, is to the following effect.

On the occasion of the state visit of George the Third to the City, on the first Lord Mayor's day after his ascension to the throne, there was considerable tumult, amounting to a riot, in the great thoroughfare from St. Paul's to the Bank. The shouts of the people, added to the dismal noises made by the creaking of the various signs over the shops—it must be remembered that the numbering of houses did not take place before 1770, the dwellings being distinguished previously by signs, such as the "Leather Bottle" of Hoare, the bankers in Fleet Street—caused one of the horses of the King's carriage to become restive, so as to cause imminent danger to the illustrious occupants.

In this emergency, a worthy Quaker and linen draper, David Barclay, seeing the Royal carriage swaying to and fro in

70

front of his door, and the King and Queen seriously upset, stepped forth into the street, and addressed George the Third. *"Wilt thee alight, George, and thy wife Charlotte, and come into my house and see the Lord Mayors Show.?"* friend Barclay bluntly inquired of the Majesty of England.

The King, who had, with many of his family, a strong partiality for Quakers—imported, probably, from the Hanoverian plains, where Herrnhuter and other sects of "Friends" are rather numerous— condescended to accept the invitation of the worthy linen draper, and went up into the first floor over the shop to see the Lord Mayor's Show. The aldermanic cavalcade having passed, David Barclay introduced the whole of his family to the King and Queen: —*"George, King of England—Priscilla Barclay, my wife;"* *"Priscilla Barclay, my wife—George, King of England,"* and so-forth. On taking his leave to proceed to Guildhall, his Majesty said, *"David, let me see thee at St. James's next Wednesday, and bring thy son John with thee."*

David did care for the invitation, and he went westward into the courtly region to please his guest of the Lord Mayor's Show. When making their appearance at the levee, David and John kept a little in the background; but the King had no sooner espied them, when, throwing aside all restraint of etiquette, he descended from the throne, and, with a hearty shake of the hand, welcomed the linen draper and his son to St. James's. After saying many kind words to both of them, he asked David Barclay what he intended to do with his son John; and, without waiting for a reply, exclaimed: — *"Let him come here, and I will provide him with honourable and profitable employment."*

The word *"profitable"* sounded pleasant enough to the ear of David; yet he was too cautious a man to jump into any wild conclusions about courtly honours. Reflecting for a moment, the Quaker, with many apologies, requested permission to refuse the Royal offer, adding: — *"I fear the air of your Majesty's court will not agree with my son."* The compliment was by no means a flattering one; yet King George was pleased, and cried in his peculiar way, *"Well, David, well, well; you know best, you know best. But you must not forget to let me see you occasionally at St. James's."*

How often the shrewd linen draper and his son went to St. James's, or whether they went at all, history does not tell: it is highly probable the road from Cheapside to Pall-mall was not frequently trodden by the two Quakers, father and son. What is sure is, that *David Barclay*, soon after rejecting the royal offer of honours, established his eldest son James, together with John, as bankers in Lombard Street, in the well-founded expectation that the thousands made in linen drapery would grow into tens and hundreds of thousands in the exercise of the art of banking. So, it happened, indeed, and in course of time *John Barclay*, who would have been certainly a bad courtier, became the intelligent founder of one of the most flourishing private banking firms of the history.

The story of George the Third's accidental visit to David Barclay's house in Cheapside is contradicted by several writers, among others by *Morris Charles Jones*, in an interesting little pamphlet, printed for private circulation, called *"Reminiscences connected with an Old Oak Panelling."* It is stated here that the King came by special invitation, the house having been prepared for him by the city entertainment committee. David Barclay's descendants subsequently became great brewers as well as bankers. David's eldest son by a second marriage—with Priscilla Freame, daughter of John Freame, banker, "near George's Yard, Lombard Street" —purchased, in concert with three partners, the large brewery established by Henry Thrale, the friend of Dr. Johnson, changing the title into the world-famous Barclay, Perkins, and Co. Subsequently, the banking and brewing firms entered into repeated connection.

On John Freame's death, without successors, the banking business came into the hands of *James Barclay*, and on the latter dying without male progenies, the institution devolved upon his two brothers, *David Barclay of Youngbury*, and *John Barclay of Cambridge Heath*. The two Barclays associated with them their cousin, *Sylvanus Bevan*, who subsequently left to join the brewing firm; and also, John Henton Tritton, who married Mary, the daughter of John Barclay. The last-named David Barclay had no son to succeed him; but John Barclay was succeeded by his son, *Robert Barclay of Clapham*, who in turn was followed by his son, John Barclay of Leyton. The last-named was succeeded by his eldest surviving son, the John Gurney Barclay, of Leyton, who had a son, Robert, also in the banking house. Although Sylvanus Bevan left the banking firm, his son, David Bevan, succeeded him therein. He, in his turn, was followed by his son, Robert Cooper Lee Bevan, a senior member of the house; who had also a son, Francis Augustus Bevan. John Henton Tritton was succeeded in his share by one of his name and blood.

The two-great banking and brewing institutions are thus constituted almost entirely of progenies of David Barclay of Cheapside, who in 1690, after the death of his father, Robert Barclay of Ury—the author of the celebrated *"Apology for the Quakers,"*— came to London with his pittance of £6,000, a Scotch younger son's fortune. He put himself a novice to James Taylor, of the company of drapers—the sign of whose house in Cheapside was the Bear—whom he succeeded, having married his daughter. So much for David Barclay, of Cheapside, who entertained royal George the Third, and all his worthy descendants. Their genealogy is really full of interest, and exemplifies the truth of Carlyle's saying: "*In these days, ten ordinary histories of kings and courtiers were well exchanged against the tenth part of one good history of booksellers.*"

The mode of conducting the business of banking, in the latter part of the eighteenth century, was very different from what it is now-a-days. The banker early attended on 'Change, which was usually over about half-past two o'clock ; he then went home to dinner, and not unfrequently to the theatre, and afterwards returned to Lombard Street to attend to his business and finish his correspondence. Late in the day, when all the letters were finished, the parcel was dispatched to the Post-office, to go by the night mail, leaving London at twelve o'clock. These midnight mails were curiosities which would astonish a modern Londoner, accustomed to railways, steamers, and express trains of forty miles an hour. The whole correspondence of the British metropolis, involving transactions of perhaps millions in value, was entrusted to a number of ragged little postboys, who carried the letters in pouches slung across the horses' back.

A curious account of this old Post-office system, in existence till the latter part of the eighteenth century, is given by the John Palmer, the Rowland Hill of his days, in the exposition of his scheme of postal reform, submitted to Mr. Pitt in 1783. "*The post at present*," says Palmer's memoir, "*instead of being the swiftest, is almost the slowest conveyance in this country; and though, from the great improvements in our roads, other carriers have proportionately mended their speed, the post is as slow as ever. It is likewise very unsafe, as the frequent robberies of it testify; and, to avoid a loss of this nature, people generally cut bank-bills, or bills at sight, in two, and send the parts by different posts. The Post-Master-General lately advertised directions to the public how to divide a bill in such a manner as to prevent its being of any use to the robber. Rewards have also been frequently offered by him for the best-constructed mail-cart, or some plan to prevent the frequent robbery of the mail, but without effect. Indeed, it is at present generally entrusted to some idle boy, without character, mounted on a worn-out hack, and who, so far from being able to defend himself, or escape from a robber, is much more likely to be in league with him.*"

## SIX MILLIONAIRE BANKERS

Towards the end of the eighteenth century, when George the Third was King, and when Meyer Amschelm kept a broker's shop in the Jew-lane of Frankfort under the sign of the Red Shield— *"Rothschild"*—there were only six bankers in London who had the repute of being possessed of extraordinary wealth, or were what is now termed millionaires. These six bankers were *Thomas Coutts, Sir Francis Baring, Joseph Denison, Henry Hope, Lewis Tessier*, and *Peter Thellusson*. Of Thomas Coutts and the interesting incidents of his early career mention has been made already, and it need be added only that he began life with a capital under a thousand, and died worth nearly a million of money.

The career of Sir Francis Baring was still more successful. Like their modern successors and rivals, the world-famous bankers of the Red Shield, the Barings came from Germany. The immediate ancestor of the family was Herr Francis Baring, pastor of the Lutheran Church at Bremen, who came over to this country in the latter part of his life His son, *John Baring*, established himself as a cloth-manufacturer at Larkbeer, in Devonshire, and by the exercise of untiring hard work gained a considerable wealth.

He left four sons, two of whom, John and Francis, came to London and set up in business as importers of wools and dye-stuffs, acting also as agents to the Larkbeer cloth factory. The elder brother, John, afterwards withdrew from business, and retired to Exeter; whereupon Francis, then sole head of the firm, wound up his old business and ventured to banking transactions. He traded mainly in Government loans, and soon became the friend and financial adviser of the Premier, Lord Shelburne, who used to style him the *"Prince of Merchants."* Shelburne's successor, William Pitt, thought it necessary to gain the goodwill of the influential banker by the gift of a baronetcy, and on the 29th of May, 1793, Mr. Baring became *Sir Francis Baring*. The founder of the great banking house—born April 18,1740—died September 12, 1810, leaving behind him a fortune estimated at above two million sterling. Francis Baring in his own person was, without comparison, the most successful accumulator of wealth of the eighteenth century.

It is not without interest to follow the fortunes of the house of Baring for another generation or two. Sir Francis Baring, by his marriage with a niece of the *Archbishop of Canterbury*, left five sons, the three eldest of whom—Thomas, Alexander, and Henry—became partners in the banking institution. Sir Thomas withdrew from business soon after the death of his father, thinking it unbecoming in a baronet to be a banker; and Henry Baring likewise retired not long after, for a very different reason.

Henry Baring was addicted to gambling, which he carried on at a high rate at the *Palais Royal*, Paris, and other famous "*hells*" of the time, where his nightly appearance, with mountains of gold and bank notes before him, was the wonder of all spectators. He was by no means an unlucky disciple of the *rouge-et-noir*; for he several times broke the "*Entreprise générale des jeux*," carrying off sums which would have been princely fortunes to any but Barings.

Notwithstanding this luck, his presence at the Continental gaming tables was naturally considered a scandal at the London banking-house of Baring Brothers, and, after some negotiation Henry Baring was induced to withdraw from the firm. There now remained as head of the institution, *Alexander Baring*, born October 27, 1774, and brought up in the House of Hope. When the Hope returned to England, in consequence of the occupation of Holland by the troops of revolutionary France, Alexander Baring left the establishment and went to the United States, where he married the eldest daughter of *William*

*Bingham*, then considered the richest man in America, and who brought him a fortune of 900,000 dollars.

Alexander Baring had no sooner become head of the house when he entered on a series of monetary operations on a gigantic scale and of European importance. The greatest of these— one of the greatest ever undertaken by a single banker— was, that he freed France from the incubus of an occupation of Russian, Prussian, and Austrian armies of 50,000 men each, by the loan of a sum of 27,238,938 francs, at 5 percent, *rentes*. This momentous transaction occasioned the saying of the witty French Premier, the Duke de Richelieu: *"There are six great Powers in Europe: England, France, Russia, Austria, Prussia, and Baring Brothers."*

Alexander Baring— *"Alexander the Great"* —died at Longleat, Wilts, on May 13, 1848, having been elevated to the peerage, under the title of Lord Ashburton, in 1835. He left four sons, the eldest of whom, William Bingham—who died in March, 1864—succeeded him in the family honours, while the second, Francis, born in May, 1800, took for a while the nominal direction of the firm. In this capacity, he engaged in some remarkable transactions. He purchased, among other things, the whole of the territory surrounding the lake Tezcuco, on the island of which stands the city of Mexico, and thus made himself, in a sense, master of the capital of a great country. The other members of the firm of *Baring and Co.*, were, however, startled by the gigantic nature of the purchase, and, after great efforts, succeeded in getting rid of the supposed Frankenstein.

Francis Baring married, in 1833, the daughter of the Duke of Bassano, Napoleon's Secretary of State, and settled at Paris, in one of the princely residences of the *Place Vendôme*, which he purchased for £64,000. By the recent death of his elder brother, Francis Baring has become Lord Ashburton, and retired from the firm, in which, for some time ago, he was only a nominal partner.

The Imperial Parliament, in the Session of 1864, counted no less than six Barings—one in the house of Lords and five in the Commons. Few families of Great Britain have risen to higher influence, both in the political and commercial world, in the course of a century, than the descendants of the humble German pastor, whom chance drove, in his declining years, from Bremen to London.

Of the six millionaire bankers of the eighteenth century, the last-named, Peter Thellusson, rose to fame in a very singular manner. Thellusson was born at Paris, in 1735, the son of M. Isaac Thellusson, a native of Geneva, who was established as banker in a good way of business. This he extended considerably by the assistance of a clerk, afterwards famous in history as M. Necker, revolutionary Minister of Finance. Mons. Isaac Thellusson, appreciating the value of his clerk, accepted him after a time into partnership, so the firm subsequently became *Thellusson and Necker*.

When Peter Thellusson had grown up into manhood, he was likewise admitted as member of the Paris firm; but the first throes of the Revolution, which were felt not long after, made him restless at his desk, and he resolved on immigrating to London, and creating a branch bank in connection with the house of Thellusson and Necker. A man of great sagacity and extraordinary determination, coupled with a desire for making money which amounted to an all-absorbing passion, Peter Thellusson found success at his door, and in a few years built up one of the first banking establishments in the British metropolis.

But, however great his wealth, he still yearned for more; and pondering day and night on this one great object of his life, he at last hit upon an extraordinary expedient for multiplying the fortune amassed by him. In April, 1796, he put his name to a last will and testament which made the house of Thellusson for ever memorable. Under this will, various legacies were left by Peter

Thellusson to his wife, his three sons and three daughters, amounting together to about £100,000.

The whole residue of his fortune, valued at above £600,000, was made over to trustees, to accumulate, and to be laid out by them in the purchase of estates in England, until such time as all his children, and the male children of his sons and grandsons should die, after which the whole property was directed to go to the nearest lineal male descendants bearing the name of Thellusson. Among these descendants, the property was then to be distributed in the following manner.

The vast estate— grown up into gigantic extents by the accumulation of interest and compound interest—was to be divided into three equal shares: the first to go to the male children of the testator's eldest son; another to the second son's male children, and the remaining to the male heirs of the third. In case of failure of male descendants of any one of the three sons, his share was to go to the other two; and if there was a failure of two, then the whole three lots were to be consolidated into one vast property, constituting by far the largest private fortune ever known in Europe, or, indeed, in the world. Finally, in the event that there should remain no lineal male descendants, the testator directed that the whole estate should be sold, and the proceeds used to pay off the national debt.

Peter Thellusson's calculations seemed correct; and evidently not the shadow of a doubt existed in his mind that by the simple accumulation of interest and compound interest, through three or four generations, his wealth would swell into dimensions compared with which the fortunes of Kings and Emperors would seem beggarly trifles. Unfortunately, the testator had left one element out of calculation— the fact of the existence of a British institution called the *Court of Chancery*, at the shrine of which live an army of learned gentlemen, all anxious to participate in the pleasing action of interest and compound interest. In July, 1797, Peter Thellusson shut his eyes, directed, no doubt, eagerly towards the future, and the countless wealth accumulating to other Thellusson for generations to come.

But after little more than a year, in December, 1798, two bills were already filed in the Court of Chancery against the will, the one by the widow and her sons and three daughters and the husbands of the two then married, and the other by the acting trustees of the bulk of the property. The validity of the will was established before the Lord Chancellor and the other judges of the Court of Chancery; nevertheless, the gentlemen of the long robe were not at all inclined to give up their valuable prize. For years and years to come, bills, applications, and injunctions *in re* Thellusson kept cropping up in the law courts; and legal miners kept digging into the wonderful estate with as hearty energy as any miners in the Australian gold-fields.

Mrs. Thellusson got sick over it, and died of a broken heart—or a broken purse—in January, 1805, seven years after her calculating husband. Her surviving family continued to act the fable of the oyster and the shell. All the three sons of Peter Thellusson had seats in the House of Commons, and the eldest, Peter Isaac Thellusson, obtained an Irish peerage, and changed into *Baron Rendlesham*. Yet, for all this, the family did not greatly prosper in the world, and having once got into the meshes of the honourable Court of Chancery, never came out of them again. Under the diligent working of the gentlemen of the long robe, the eighty or hundred million sterling which Peter Thellusson had calculated upon for his great-great-grandchildren, dwindled down to very modest proportions, not at all conspicuous among the thousands of first-class fortunes at present assessed to the income-tax.

There were no more millionaire Thellussons; no more members of the family in Parliament; and no more banking institutions bearing the famous name. Peter Thellusson, besides overlooking the Court of Chancery, made one fundamental mistake in his calculation. He did not remember, or perhaps did not know, that large wealth has not only to be acquired, but must also be kept together, by active human brains and industrious human hands. Interest and compound interest alone will not do it.

Peter Thellusson (1850–1899), on Board the Yacht, 'Albion'", c. 1894, by George Percy Jacomb-Hood (British, 1857-1929). Thellusson is shown smartly dressed but relaxed on board his steam yacht, the 'Albion'.

# THE BANKERS OF RED SHIELD

Right in the center of ancient city of Frankfort-on-the-Maine there is a narrow, wretched-looking lane, formed by tall, dark houses, with dirty windows and dirtier doors, with a population more ragged than that of the Seven Dials. This miserable thoroughfare is called the *Judengasse* or Jew-lane; and in one of its dark houses, the number 148, the founder of eminent house of Rothschild was born. When Meyer Amschel saw the light of the world in 1743, the Jew-lane was a prison, guarded by heavy chain at either end, which were fastened every evening, as well as on all Sundays, holidays, and festivals of Church, and out of this prison the wretched dwellers durst not stir, under penalty of death. No Jew was allowed under any circumstances to live beyond the limits of *Judengasse*; which obligated the unfortunate outcasts to raise their black, sunless houses higher and higher every subsequent generation, or else to hide themselves away in deep crypts under the ground. Such were the early environs that greeted the founder of Rothschild banking family.

Meyer Amschel – or, as he was afterwards called, *Anselm*–lost both his parents at the age of eleven, and had to fight his way through life single-handed, in much bitterness of heart. After attending school for a few years, he marches stick in hand and sack on his shoulders, to the city of Hanover, where he was fortunate enough to find a place as clerk to a small banker and money changer. By dint of extreme frugality, he managed to save out of his salary a little, and returned to *Frankfurter Judengasse*. Now a family man, Anselm setup the business as broker, money-lender, and trader in old coins at *Frankfurter Judengasse*.

As a skillful and shrewd collector of coins, he became popular, which brought more than one lover of numismatic curiosities into the dark shop at No. 148, which was marked with the handing sign of Red Shield –in German, *Rothschild*. Among the connoisseurs thus brought into connection with Meyer Anselm was a small German potentate, the Landgrave William of Hesse, afterwards Elector of Hesse, under the title of William I.

Those were bad times for German princes; the storms of the French Revolution and the subsequent hostilities of the great Republic making their tenure very uncertain and their incomes perilous. Landgrave William, too, had often occasion to throw away family-jewels for cash, and maybe to borrow little extra sums to satisfy insistent creditors. In this way Prince William and Meyer Anselm became close: which was a good thing both for Prince William and Meyer Anselm. When the French troops marched upon Frankfort, in 1796, the possessor of the Red Shield had time to put his chattels under the security of William's Schloss, at Cassel; a favour the banker was enabled to return with interest ten years later. The event is worth noting, as marking the starting-point of the treasures of the house of Rothschild.

Bombings of cities are not, as a rule, reckoned happy events; yet Kleber's barrage of Frankfort, in 1796, had some useful significances. The whole old Jew-lane, with all its gloomy tenements, was bashed to pieces, and the occupants had to move from among the ruins, pleading shelter from their Christian brethren. The "brethren," at first, were not much inclined to act the Good Samaritan; and the Calvinist clergy in particular seemed anxious to drive the infidels back to their Ghetto, even at the risk of their perishing among the flames.

Fortunately, the Jews by this time had some influential and obligated friends among the rulers of the city, through whom approval was bestowed them to leave the *Judengasse*, and to buy and lease, under certain limitations, houses built for Christians. The approval, coming in the wake of the French bombing, was made use of pretty largely, to the great advantage of the enterprising Hebrews. Hereafter, the Red Shield hovered in a line with the signs of the prominent money-changers of the city, and Landgrave William nominated Meyer Anselm his Hof-agent— that is, his foreign banker. The appointment led directly to the notable event which raised the family of the Rothschilds from a low position to the very highest prominence. In 1806, Landgrave William of Hesse was driven from his states by the Emperor Napoleon, who required the territory for his merry brother Jerome, whom he had just appointed King of Westphalia.

The poor Landgrave, in his great hurry, had no time to gather his cash, which he left in the hands of his Hof-agent, Meyer Anselm, thinking that it would, at any rate, be safer there than in the unrestricted pockets of the new Westphalian majesty. The sum amounted to some three million florins, or about £250,000, all in good coin of the dominion, unmixed with base paper and worthless scrip. How to take care of this money and make it grow in his hands, by ever-returning interest, was what Meyer Anselm understood to perfection.

In the hard piping times of war, money was worth twelve and even twenty percent on very good security; and many were the freeholds that went mortgaged into the shop of the Red Shield, often for less than one-third their value, never to be redeemed again. Thus, in about six years, Meyer Anselm, now called *Herr Meyer Anselm Rothschild*, very nearly quadrupled his capital; and when he died, September 13, 1812, he was held to be worth twelve million florins, or a million sterling. Shortly after this event, there followed the battle of Leipzig; peace was restored to Germany, and the *Landgrave of Hesse* returned to his states.

His serene highness had not been many days at his capital, when the eldest son of Meyer Anselm presented himself at court, handing over the three million florins which his father had taken care of Landgrave William was almost beside himself for joy at the sight of all the money. It seems he had never expected to get it back, and therefore looked upon it as a complete "*windfall.*" In his exultation, he knighted the young Rothschild at once. "Such honesty," he exclaimed, "had never before been known in the world."

At the Congress of Vienna, to which the Landgrave went shortly after, he talked of nothing but the trustworthiness of the Meyer Anselm family, making all the crowned heads of Europe emulous to entrust their savings to the bankers of the Red Shield. And the generous Hebrews of Frankfort were quite willing to take charge of all the cash, on the same terms as the money of the Landgrave —that is, *no interest.*

Meyer Anselm Rothschild left ten children, five sons and five daughters. The sons were, Anselm, born June 12, 1773; Salomon, born September 9, 1774; Nathan, born September 16, 1777; Charles, born April 24, 1788; and James, born May 15, 1792. By the will of their father, which the five sons had sworn at his deathbed to obey faithfully, they entered into co-partnership, at the same time establishing branches of the Frankfort Bank at the principal capitals of Europe.

Anselm, the eldest son, was to be the head of the firm, directing all its operations, and, if necessary, controlling the actions of his brothers. However, this arrangement was not strictly carried out; and though Anselm remained all his life the nominal head, his younger brother, Nathan, who had inherited the spirit of the father, was the real chief of the house.

In his enthusiasm to make his way in the world, that is, to make money, Nathan left his home at the early age of twenty-two, and in 1798 opened a small shop as banker and money-lender at Manchester. He had left Frankfort—where his father had just removed from the Jew-lane, knocked into ruins by brave Marshal Kleber—with only a thousand florins, or about £84, in his pocket; and with this small sum, which must have been still reduced by travelling expenses, however modest, he set up his Manchester business. At the end of five years, in 1803, Nathan came from Manchester to London, worth £200,000.

The fame of his skill in financial operations— the art of making near a quarter of a million in five years was rare even then—had come before young Rothschild, and he found numerous friends at the Exchange, particularly among Jewish community. Nathan involved principally in speculations in the public funds, his great shrewdness, and almost intuitive perception in judging of the state of the money-market, enabling him at all times to amass vast profits. An instance of his sound calculation, which proven an event of the greatest importance in his successful career, was his first transaction with the British Government.

In 1810, during the period when the fortunes of the Peninsular war seemed most doubtful, some draughts of Wellington, amounting in the aggregate to a considerable sum, came over to this country, and there was no money to meet them in the Exchequer. Nathan Rothschild, calculating, with habitual shrewdness, the chances of England's victory in her great contest against the arms of France, purchased the bills at a considerable discount, and, having made them over to the Government at par, furnished the money for redeeming them.

It was a splendid speculation in every respect, and, according to Nathan's own confession, one of the best he ever made. Henceforth the ministry entered into frequent and cherished relations with the New Hebrew banker, who fully realized the pecuniary advantages which this connection brought him. Every piece of early news which he obtained valued him the gain of thousands at the Stock Exchange, the manipulation of which he had mastered to an unexampled degree.

Soon, however, even the information which the resources of the Government furnished him, was deemed insufficient by the enterprising speculator, and he set to invent means of his own for obtaining news, far more perfect than those at the service of the Government. For this purpose, he organized a staff of active agents, whose duty it was to follow in the wake of the continental armies, and to send daily, or, if necessary, hourly reports of the most important movements, successes, or defeats, in ciphers, hidden under the wings of carrier-pigeons.

To the breed of these pigeons, *Nathan Rothschild* attached the greatest importance, and often paid large sums for birds of superior strength and swiftness. Embarking deeper and deeper in speculations on the success of the English arms, Nathan often got dissatisfied even with the speed of his winged messengers, and on more than one occasion hurried over to the Continent himself to watch the state of affairs and the progress of warlike operations. When Napoleon returned from the Isle of Elba, his anxiety knew no bounds, and during the Hundred Days he went to Belgium, following in the wake of Wellington's army. Eager to gather the earliest information of events, which, he felt, would settle the fate of Europe for years to come, he did not even shrink from the perils of the field of battle.

On the morning of the 18th of June, 1815, Nathan Rothschild rode, on a quiet horse, hired at Brussels, over the ground in front of the *Château d'Hougoumont*, close to the village of Waterloo. He was in company with a number of men well worth noticing. The foremost was the Duke of Wellington, riding his chestnut charger Copenhagen, stern of aspect, his eagle eyes measuring the field in front for miles around, up to the hillock of Rossomme, where, at a table placed upon a mattress, sat a warrior before whose name Europe trembled.

Behind the Duke, and nearer to Nathan Rothschild, were a number of diplomatic gentlemen; among them *Count Pozzo di*

*Borgo*, Baron Vincent, General Alava, Baron Muffling, and others. The banker kept close to the German Baron, eagerly inquiring after the chances of the coming struggle. It was uncertain, alas! and the fate of the English army and of the house of Rothschild hung in the balance together.

All day long, on the memorable 18th of June, Nathan Rothschild stood on the hill of Hougoumont to watch the progress of the great battle. He saw the French lines advance and retreat; and again, advance and again retreat: Napoleon all the while sitting on his mattress on the hill of Rossomme, with a large map outstretched before him. Napoleon Bonaparte on the hill of Rossomme; Nathan Rothschild on the hill of Hougoumont—the picture would be worth painting. From noon till six at night the whole field was enveloped in thick, white smoke, and when it blew off at last the troops of the French Emperor were seen in full retreat. It was near sunset; and Nathan perceived at a glance that the great battle of Waterloo was won—was won for him. Without losing a moment, Nathan spurred his horse and rode off to Brussels. Here a carriage was ready to convey him to Ostend.

At the break of day on the 19th June, Nathan Rothschild found himself at the coast opposite to England; but separated from the Thames and the Stock Exchange by a fungus sea and waves dashing mountains high. In vain the banker offered five hundred, six thousand, and eight hundred francs, to be carried across the straits from Ostend to Deal or Dover. At last he cried that he would give two thousand francs, and the bargain was struck, a poor fisherman risking his life to gain eighty pounds for his wife and children.

The frail bark which carried Caesar and his fortune sped swiftly over the waves, a sudden change of wind to the east accelerating the progress to an unexpected degree. The sun was still on the horizon when Nathan Rothschild landed at Dover, and, without waiting, engaged the swiftest horses to carry him onward to the metropolis. There was gloom in Thread-needle Street, and gloom in all men's hearts; but gloomier than any looked Nathan Rothschild when he appeared on the morning of the 20th June, leaning against his usual pillar at the Stock Exchange. He whispered to a few of his most intimate friends that Field Marshal Blucher, with his 117,000 Prussians, had been defeated by Napoleon in the great battle of Ligny, fought during the 16th and 17th of June—Heaven only knew what had become of the handful of men under Wellington! The dismal news spread like wildfire, and there was a tremendous fall in the funds.

Nathan Rothschild's *"known agents"* sold with the rest, more worried than any to get rid of their stock—but Nathan Rothschild's *"unknown agents"* bought every scrip of paper that was to be had, and left not off buying till the evening of the following day. It was only in the afternoon of the 21st of June, nearly two days after the arrival of Nathan in England, that the news of the great battle and victory of Waterloo, and the utter rout of the Napoleonic host, got known. Nathan Rothschild, radiant with joy, was the first to inform his friends at the Stock Exchange of the happy event, spreading the news a quarter of an hour before it was given to the general public. Needless to say, that the rates rose faster than they had fallen, as soon as the official reports were published of the great battle of Waterloo.

Waterloo enriched the house of Rothschild by about a million sterling, and laid the foundation of a European power for the descendants of Meyer Amschel, the poor broker of Frank-fort-on-the-Main.

The "House of the Red Shield", the Rothschild house, was very probably one of those on the right. This is Judengasse, (Jews Lane or Jews Alley), in Frankfurt's Altstadt (old town). Photo / Richard H. Jones

The House of the Red Shield (Rothschild) and The House of the Ship in Old Frankfurt. Although under one roof, was divided into two. The left side being the nest of the Rothschilds humble beginnings in international banking.

## NATHAN ROTHSCHILD'S FINAL CAREER.

Having gained their first couple of millions, honours and dignities rained fast upon the Rothschild family. The Emperor of Austria, in 1815, made all the five brothers hereditary-nobles, and, seven years after, elevated them to the rank of *Freiherr*, or Baron, which title they still bear. The career of Nathan, after the battle of Waterloo, continued to be eminently prosperous. He made money even in speculations that turned out bad, such as the English loan of twelve million, for which he became responsible in 1819, and which fell to a discount; but not before Nathan had relieved himself of all liability. But his greatest successes were in international lending, which he was the first to make popular in England by introducing the payment of dividends, which formerly took place abroad, in the London market, and fixing the rate in sterling pound.

Dating from about 1819, the transactions of Nathan Rothschild were spread over the entire globe. He negotiated loans with the Czar of Russia, as well with South American Republics; and made deals at the same time with the Pope of Rome and the Turkish Sultan. Nothing seemed too gigantic for his grasp; nothing too minute for his notice. But while investing the profits of a bargain of ten million, and purchasing an estate of £115,000 with the premium of a single foreign loan, he at the same time calculated to a penny the wages on which a clerk was able to live—say a clerk at Camberwell with a wife and seven children, and meat once a week.

It was characteristic of Nathan that he never paid his employees a farthing more than was necessary for their bare subsistence; or at least not a farthing more than they could compel him to pay. This meanness towards those who assisted him in building up the edifice of his enormous fortune, is a reproach to the character of the man, from which even his warmest adulators have not been able to free him.

Notwithstanding his avarice in ordinary life, Nathan Rothschild was fond of showing his wealth in luxurious entertainments and sumptuous banquets, to which he invited the aristocracy of rank and birth—though not that of talent Peers and princes of the blood sat at his table; bishops and archbishops bowed before him; and those who preached loudest against Mammon were foremost in worshipping the successful representative of the golden guinea. At his grand entertainments, Nathan, who was really a very uneducated man, and scarcely able to write, covered his ignorance by an affected bluntness of speech and manner which, though it imposed on some, made him extremely ludicrous in the eyes of others.

Thus, he was a constant mark for the satirists of the day. His huge and slovenly appearance; the lounging attitude he assumed when leaning against his pillar at the Royal Exchange; his rugged speech, with strongly marked Jewish accent and idiom, made caricature easy, and gave him up as helpless victim to his enemies. Of these he had many; some of them created, no doubt, by envy; but also, a large number of others whom he had ruined, or who fancied themselves ruined by him. Few weeks passed in the latter part of his career without his receiving threatening letters, informing him that unless he should deposit a certain sum of money at a given place, he would be shot, or poisoned, or, more liberally, blown up in his house in Piccadilly.

These threats at times took such an effect upon Nathan Rothschild as to haunt him like a nightmare. One day, two tall, mustachioed men —it must be remembered that this was the anti-mustachioed period—were shown into the private parlour at the St. Swithin's Lane counting-house. Nathan bowed; the visitors bowed. Nathan arose; and his bearded visitors moved close up to him, their hands fumbling about in the pockets of their great-coats. Nathan saw it at a glance—the mustachioed fellows had come to shoot him, their hands searching for weapons in their pockets. Quick as lightning, Nathan took up his brass-bound ledger and hurled it at the heads of the strangers, at the same time screaming "Murder!" in a paroxysm of fright. The screams brought all the clerks and porters of the house into his sanctum.

Explanations took place, when it was found that the two mustachioed strangers were bankers from abroad, who, with a little nervous anxiety in the presence of the Caesar of the Stock Exchange, had fumbled in their pockets for letters of introduction and other necessary credentials. — "You must be a happy man, Mr. Rothschild," said once a gentleman, sitting at Nathan's banqueting table, and glancing around at the superb appointments of the mansion of his host. "Happy! —me happy!" was the reply. "What! Happy, when just as you are going to dine you have a letter placed in your hands, saying, 'If you do not send me £500, I will blow your brains out?' Happy! me happy!"— Instead of with his wife, Nathan frequently slept with a pair of loaded pistols by his side.

In 1831, Nathan Rothschild did a stroke of business which, while it brought him and his house immense profits, also heaped upon them not a little obloquy, freely expressed in many English and foreign newspapers. The business consisted in an attempt to get the monopoly of the sale of mercury. It is well known that the supply of mercury is exceedingly limited, being, in fact, almost entirely drawn from two mines, those of Almaden, in Spain, and of Idria, near Adelsberg, in Illyria. The mines of Almaden, which were known to the Greeks seven hundred years before Christ, and which furnished 700,000 pounds' weight annually to Rome during the Imperial era, fell somewhat into neglect at the commencement of the nineteenth century, on account of the Napoleonic wars, so that the Spanish Government derived less profit from them than formerly.

Under these circumstances, when the ministers of his Catholic Majesty were hard up for funds, in 1831, they entertained the application of Nathan Rothschild to furnish them with a loan, on condition of the Almaden mines being made over to him for a number of years as security. The bargain was struck, and the house of Rothschild entered in possession of the mines, commencing the business by immediately doubling the price of Almaden mercury. The commercial world, much astonished at this step, addressed itself to Idria; when it was discovered that the mines of Idria had passed likewise, very quietly, into the hands of Nathan Rothschild, who had settled, of course, the price of the mercury on the same scale as that of Almaden.

By this little transaction, the house of Rothschild obtained a complete monopoly of the sale of mercury, and the head of the firm was able to settle the price of the commodity, indispensable for many purposes, at his counting house in St. Swithin's Lane, without fear of competition. This clever stroke of business— as profitable as it was clever—had one notable consequence for the sick and suffering of all nations.

Mercurial preparations, largely employed in medicine, are, at the present moment, no more manufactured from the pure metal as obtained from the mines, but from the refuse of other articles containing quicksilver, such as the foil of old mirrors and looking-glasses. It would be interesting, if the statistics were given, to calculate how many pounds sterling the house of Rothschild made by the little mercury business, and how many persons died in consequence of bad mercurial medicines.

The guiding principle in all the affairs of the house of Rothschild was the co-partnership of its members, enjoined on his deathbed by Meyer Anselm, the founder of the house. To strengthen this bond of union, Nathan conceived the idea of establishing blood-alliances between the various members of his family, not only in his own time, but for succeeding generations.

Accordingly, in 1836, he summoned a family congress to Frankfort-on-the-Maine, to deliberate on this important addition to the laws of the house, and to take measures for the development of the plan.

The congress was to be inaugurated by the marriage of two first-cousins of the family, namely, the eldest son of Nathan with the eldest daughter of his brother Charles. Nathan arrived at Frankfort in best health and spirits, exceedingly Joyful that his great plan, which placed the house of Rothschild on the same basis as the reigning families of Europe, was so near its execution.

The marriage of Lionel de Rothschild to his cousin Charlotte took place with due pomp, on the 15th of June, 1836, at the Frankfort synagogue—within a stone's throw of the dark old dwelling in the Jew-lane, the early residence of Meyer Anselm, and still inhabited by his aged wife. But on the very same day Nathan fell ill, and he being nigh sixty years of age, it was suggested that his physician, Mr. Travers, should be sent for at once from London. But the great man would not listen to this advice. Physicians, he said, were very expensive luxuries—too expensive for a man possessing a bare three or four million.

A cheap medical adviser was called in accordingly, under whose hands Nathan grew rapidly worse, Mr. Travers at last was summoned by the family; but he came too late. On the 26th of July, Nathan grew delirious, talking incoherently of pounds, florins, and thalers; and on the 28th he was a corpse. Early on the morning of the 2gth of July, an amateur sportsman, looking out for birds in the neighbourhood of Brighton, shot a pigeon, which, when picked up, proved to be one of the well-known carrier pigeons of the house of Rothschild. It had, however, no letters concerning loans and the state of the money market under its wings, but only a small bit of paper with the inscription "*Il est mort*"—he is dead. Who the he was, there could be no doubt.

That day there was a complete panic at the Stock Exchange, and a great fall in the funds.

The remains of Nathan Rothschild were brought over from Frankfort to England, and he was buried with great pomp at the Jewish East-end cemetery, on the 8th of August, 1836. Previous to burial, the coffin—which, according to the newspapers of the day, "*was different in shape to those made in this country, and so handsomely carved and decorated with large silver handles at both sides and ends that it appeared more like a cabinet, or splendid piece of furniture, than a receptacle for the dead*"—was exhibited in the counting-house, at New Court, St. Swithin's Lane, the chief scene of Nathan's financial triumphs.

The body of the great millionaire was followed to the grave by a file of mourning carriages nearly a mile in length. Among the "mourners" were the Austrian, Russian, Prussian, Neapolitan, and Portuguese ambassadors, besides the Lord Mayor, sheriffs, and aldermen, and a host of minor dignitaries. Public curiosity, after the funeral was over, was very intense on the subject as to what amount of property Nathan Rothschild had left behind him. While some stated it at three, others made it six million, and some even fabled of ten.

The will, which was soon after published, left this curiosity ungratified, for it furnished no account whatever of the amount of Nathan's property, nor of the securities in which it was invested. In the will, the executors, consisting of the four brothers of the deceased, his widow, one of his sons, his son-in-law, and Benjamin Cohen, his brother-in-law, were strictly prohibited from prying into or interfering with anything in their official capacity, beyond the line of their prescribed duties as administrators.

The statement of a co-partnership between the descendants of Meyer Anselm was, however, distinctly made in the will. Nathan, after declaring that he had an interest in all the houses conducted by his brothers on the Continent, ordered that his four sons should carry on the joint business as heretofore, in conjunction with their uncles. To his three daughters, Nathan left £000,000 each; but under the strict condition that they should marry with the consent of their mother and brothers. In the contrary case, they were to receive nothing. The same highly-disciplined generosity distinguished the remaining part of the will of Nathan Rothschild. To public charities, servants, or dependents, not a penny was left by the owner of millions.

# THE PILLARS OF THE STOCK EXCHANGE

Considering that, as it is stated on high authority, the English are a nation of Shopkeepers, it seems very strange that in one of the most important branches of shopkeeping, the barter in money, leading men have always been foreigners. From the time that the first Italians established themselves in Lombard Street, down to the advent of Nathan, the son of Meyer Amschel, foreigners have dealt largest in money, foreigners have been the highest speculators in cash and scrip, and foreigners have made the greatest fortunes in this traffic. Foreigners, in fact, have been the pillars of the Stock Exchange. With very few exceptions, all those who ever amassed great wealth by dealing in money, were either aliens or of foreign extraction. The Barings came from Germany; the Thellussons from France; and three other famous gatherers of millions, Rothschild, Goldsmid, and Sampson Gideon, were Jews.

The history of the last-named great banker and stockbroker forms a very interesting episode in the history of the Stock Exchange. In one respect, Sampson Gideon was more successful than Nathan Rothschild, for while the family of the latter did not rise in social distinction higher than to a poor Austrian barony, that of the former scaled up into the seventh heaven of the British peerage. Sampson, the Croesus of the Stock Exchange towards the end of the eighteenth century, and intimate friend of Sir Robert Walpole, was a shrewd, sarcastic man, possessed of a rich vein of humor, noble and generous in all affairs of ordinary life, and in every respect the counterpart of his famous successor of the Red Shield.

There are a good many anecdotes of the first "*great Jew broker*," some of them rather characteristic of his life and times. In one of his dealings with Mr. Snow, the banker—immortalized by Dean Swift— Gideon had occasion to borrow £20,000. Very shortly afterwards a panic occurred, and Mr. Snow, alarmed for the safety of his loan, addressed a piteous epistle to the Jew, entreating him to pay the money at once, and thereby to save him from bankruptcy and utter ruin.

Gideon knew his man well, and determined to give him back the coveted property, but to punish him at the same time for his want of confidence. So, he sent for a phial of hart's horn, and, wrapping it in twenty notes of £1,000 each, returned the loan in this form to "*Mr. Thomas Snow, goldsmith, near Temple Bar.*" Gideon was active in establishing one of the early insurance and annuity societies, in the welfare of which he took an active part, not unmixed with occasional droll behaviour. "Never grant life annuities to old women," he would say, "they wither but they never die;" and if the proposed candidate approached with a violent asthmatic cough, he perhaps called out, "*Ay, ma'am, you may cough, but it shan't save you six months' purchase.*" Under all this rough, unfriendly outside, Sampson Gideon hid a kindly heart.

He educated all his children in the Christian faith, but was unwilling himself to change his religion. He pleaded that he was too stiff and old; observing wisely that change of religion is a foolish and unproductive affair at a time when life is turning into the sere and yellow leaf but he was anxious, nevertheless, that his sons should become good Christians, and, with this view, he used to examine them himself in the tenets of faith. At these periodical examinations, Sampson sometimes went a little out of his depth, and questions were put and answers given which would shock the orthodoxy alike of Jew and Christian.

One day, probing his son on the progress made in his religious studies, Sampson put to the hopeful young Christian the query, "Who made you?" The prompt answer was, "God." And next, "Who redeemed you" to which the proper reply was given. Old Sampson now got fidgety; he knew he had to put a third question, but had clean forgotten the text. So in his embarrassment, he stammered out, "And who—who—who gave you that hat?" Whereupon young hopeful shouted with great energy, "The Holy Ghost." Through the influence of Sampson with Walpole, this exemplary young Christian was created a baronet at the age of eleven, and advanced to the dignity of an Irish baron soon after he had reached manhood.

Old Sampson desired his son should be called Sir Sampson Gideon; but the young nobleman did not relish his Scriptural name, and, after his father's death, changed his appellation into Sir S. G. Eardley, having obtained the latter name from a marriage with the daughter of Sir John Eardley Wilmot, Lord Chief Justice of the Court of Common Pleas. Old Sampson died in 1762, having amassed a fortune valued at nearly a million. "Gideon is dead," says one of the writers of the day, "*worth more than the whole land of Canaan. He has left the reversion of all his milk and honey, after his son and daughter, and their children, to the Duke of Devonshire, without insisting on the duke taking his name or being circumcised.*"

The contrast of the great Jew broker of the eighteenth century with Nathan Rothschild is strikingly shown in the will of the former, by which he left £1,000 to the synagogue of his countrymen; £1,000 to the London Hospital; and £2,000 besides an annual donation, to the Sons of the Clergy, Sampson's son, the first Lord Eardley, a very eccentric man, squandered a good deal of the money gained by his sire in political and electioneering jobs, and was also vain enough to spend large sums in the attempt to marry his children into "old families." There came not much, after all, of this desire to gain ancestral honours for the Gideons. A third little Sampson saw the light of the world in 1770, and grew up into a Lord Eardley; but he was destined to be the last of his race.

Since 1824, the title of Baron Eardley is enrolled in the big genealogical books among the lists of "Dormant and Extinct Peerages of Great Britain and Ireland." A branch of the Eardleys, indistinctly connected with the great Hebrew trunk, is, however, still extant, though it cannot be said that it still "flourishes." On the 2nd of June, 1864, as recorded in the daily papers, a batch of proclamations of outlawry was delivered at the Sheriffs' Court, Red Lion Square, and among the names in the list figured "Sir Eardley Gideon Culling Eardley, Baronet, at the suit of Robert Morris."

This is the last glimmer of publicity of the descendants of Sampson Gideon, the rich Hebrew broker. Croesus and friend of Walpole in the eighteenth—outlaw, "at the suit of Robert Morris," in the nineteenth century! Considering that a million sterling in five-pound bank-notes, closely compressed, would form a higher pile than the Monument near London Bridge, one might have thought that the fortune left by Sampson Gideon would have lasted his descendants more than a hundred years— at least have kept them somewhat longer from that fatal Sheriffs' Court in the square of the Red Lion.

The trio of wealthy Hebrew bankers and bill-brokers, pillars of the Stock Exchange, is completed by the brothers Goldsmid. At the beginning of the present century, there was scarcely a firm of higher standing in all England than that of Abraham and Benjamin Goldsmid. The two brothers esteemed as much on account of their integrity, uprightness, and often generosity, as because of their boundless success in accumulating a vast fortune. They started from the very smallest beginning.

In early life, Abraham and Benjamin Goldsmid kept a common broker's shop in Goodman's Fields, which business proving very lucrative, they ventured further, and, in 1792, set up as money-lenders and stock-brokers in Capel Court, opposite the

Bank. Here the brothers made the acquaintance of Mr. Abraham New-land, chief cashier of the *Bank of England* — whose name, figuring at the bottom of the national paper currency for more than half a century, was for a long time something like a "household word" in the country—and through him they rose at once to the pinnacle of stock-broking activity. During the whole of Newland's career, there were incessant Government loans, brought on by the pressure of war, and it was an established rule that a certain amount of each loan was always reserved for the cashier of the *Bank of England.*

A Parliamentary report names £100,000 as the sum on one occasion; perhaps it was more on others; at any rate, it was always a good round sum, and, what was better, always a most profitable investment, as the loan generally came out at a premium. Abraham Newland, the great man, took a liking to the brothers Goldsmid, and ended by making them his financial agents. Starting under such auspices, with the aid of their own superior intelligence, thrift, and foresight, their success was rapid. In 1801, they became, for the first time, contractors for a portion of the Government loan of five million, the deal was proven so lucrative that, at the next loan, they were enabled to treble their previous subscription. In this way, at the end of five or six years, the brothers amassed an immense fortune, variously estimated at from £600,000 to £800,000.

Imbued with innate love of show, and fondness for society, the Goldsmids spent their wealth as freely as they had won it. They subscribed thousands to philanthropic and charitable undertakings; they built themselves mansions vying in splendour with royal palaces; they entertained the aristocracy of birth, rank, and talent at gorgeous banquets, and they altogether lived in a style of magnificence scarcely equaled by the most distinguished personages in the kingdom. This career of luxury, if not of ostentation, was suddenly cut short in the most tragic manner.

On the nth of April, 1808, Benjamin Goldsmid, the younger of the two brothers, went to bed in usual health and spirits, at his splendid country seat at Roehampton. The possessor of enormous wealth, of a charming wife to whom he was most fondly attached, and of seven beloved children, who could be a happier man than Benjamin Goldsmid? But the happy man went to rest on the evening of the 11th, and on the following morning his servant found him suspended from the tester of his bed. The case was duly reported in the newspapers, and they agreed in a body, that Benjamin Goldsmid had committed suicide. But what could have driven the prosperous and seemingly happy man to this desperate act, nobody could tell. The twelve wise men, representatives of the *vox populiy* sat, as usual, in solemn coroner's conclave, to decide upon the cause of death; and, as usual, came to the easy conclusion that it was "temporary insanity."

The explanation was sufficient to an easy-going world; but it seemed insufficient to Abraham Goldsmid, who mourned and fretted over the loss of his dearly-beloved brother as if part of his own self had gone. Indeed, it was a part, if not of his physical, at least of his mental being that had departed with his brother. So, intimate had been all the relations of the two members of the house of Goldsmid, that the firm, reduced to one, was unable to do its accustomed work. Formerly invariably successful in its vast dealings and vaster speculations, the house of Goldsmid now came to be almost invariably unsuccessful.

Soon calamities crowded upon one another, and, driven to despair, Abraham Goldsmid staked at last the remaining part of his great fortune upon one card. Together with Mr. Francis Baring, he became contractor for the Government loan of fourteen million, issued in 1810. Contrary to all expectation the stock fell, and continued falling for some time. By the middle of September, 1810, Abraham's losses amounted to above £250,000, and still the prices kept sinking every day. On the evening of the 28th September, the "*omnium*" had fallen to six and a half percent, discount.

Abraham Goldsmid, that evening, came home very excited from the City to his private residence at Morden, Surrey. He sat down to dinner, however, in apparent good humor, and even joined in a party at cards. But at half-past seven, he walked from his house into the garden, passing over a bridge leading to a part of the grounds called the Wilderness. The sound of a pistol was heard soon after from this spot, and when the alarmed servants hurried up, they found their master stretched on the ground, a shot, fired by his own hand, having penetrated the head. The news of this pistol-shot at Morden created a panic in the City the next morning, and "omnium" fell from six and a half to eleven and a half percent, discount. A hundred fortunes went to pieces under the fall of the most trusted pillar of the Stock Exchange.

# EARLY SCOTCH BANKERS

It is a somewhat singular fact that as banking sprang, in the first instance, out of ordinary-mercantile and manufacturing transactions, such as the traffic in gold and silver ware, it has shown a tendency, in modern times, to return to the source from whence it came. The first English Baring was a cloth manufacturer in Devonshire; his successors, for three generations, were simple bankers; but the firm, have again become *"general merchants,"* dealing, however, with nations more than with individuals. It is, on the whole, a very natural process, thoroughly justified by the course of events.

Scarcity of capital, before the age of universal commerce— more accurately speaking, before the age of roads —concentrated all transferable wealth within the hands of a few goldsmiths, money-lenders, bankers, or whatever else they were called; they in their turn, acting as agents between labour and capital, employed the trust for fostering trade and commerce; till, in the last stage, trade and commerce took such an extension as to draw within its circle the distributors of wealth themselves.

It is a curious movement, and a most important one in the history of the last few centuries; and though there are those who look with great distrust upon such gigantic trade-banking institutions, it must be confessed that these organizations were quite in keeping with the immense development which the progress of science, devoted to the means of perfecting movement and creating a rapid intercourse between individuals as well as nations, has given to modern life. At any rate, it is highly interesting to follow, in one or two individual instances, the course of this commercial movement, which, operating upon things and people, changes the trader into a banker and the banker finally again into a trader.

In England, the first bankers were *goldsmiths*; but in Scotland they were, in a great many instances, tradesmen of a very different class, such as *drapers*, *haberdashers*, and *corndealers*. Of the many firms risen to eminence from these quests, the old *house of Coutts*—the trunk, so to speak, of the English and other Coutts—is the most remarkable. The founder of the house was *Patrick Coutts*, a native of *Montrose*, who settled at Edinburgh at the beginning of the eighteenth century. He carried on mercantile speculations with France, Holland, and America, by which he amassed a wealth of about £30,000, a substantial amount in those days. After the death of Patrick Coutts, his son John carried on the business, extending it markedly, and taking a cousin as partner.

Their business was dealing in corn, buying and selling goods on commission, and the negotiation of bills of exchange on London, Holland, France, Italy, Spain, and Portugal. The latter part of the business was a very profitable one, so that *John Coutts* grew rapidly rich, and was chosen *Lord Provost of Edinburgh* in consequence. He distinguished himself in this capacity, by setting up as the first Lord Provost who entertained public guests at his own house, it having been the custom previously to do the honours of the city at some convenient tavern or alehouse. Unfortunately, these hospitalities led the worthy merchant into excesses of the table, to which he succumbed in 1750, at the age of fifty-one.

This brought the third generation of Coutts on the stage—corn merchants and commission agents, gradually coming to be bankers. The two sons of *John Coutts*, Patrick and Thomas, on whom devolved the business of the father, were not yet able clearly to discern the advantages resulting from banking. They knew that their bill transactions were very profitable, and they even went so far as to hold money on trust from individuals, and to invest it in securities of various kinds, to the advantage of both their clients and themselves; yet they held to corn-dealing as the principal business, only puttering a little now and then in smuggled goods—tea, spirits, tobacco, and the like. To assist in defrauding his Majesty's revenue was held a perfectly legitimate matter, as is well known, in the "*good old times*."

The way in which the firm of Patrick and Thomas Coutts carried on their business, in the middle of the 19th century, an interesting account is given in the private "*Memoirs of a Banking House*," drawn up from the manuscript of Sir William Forbes, the subsequent head of the establishment. Half bankers and half corn-dealers, the brothers Coutts had a large number of clients for whom they held money in trust or for whom they negotiated bills, and the whole of these, often very important transactions, were carried on in a couple of small rooms, on the second floor of a house in Parliament Close, Edinburgh.

This very unostentatious tenement also formed the residence of the two brothers, and from here likewise they directed their transactions in corn, which were on a considerable scale. They had a settled agent in *Northumberland*, who was employed to make purchases for the company; and they had a great many other commission agents in the leading agricultural districts of England and Scotland.

Among the latter, number was a somewhat celebrated character, a *Cooper Thornhill*, who at that time kept the *Bell Inn*, at Stilton. Master Thornhill travelled at railway speed forty years prior to the birth of *George Stephenson*. His greatest achievement in this respect was a ride from Stilton to London, back to Stilton, and thence to London again, the whole distance being 225 miles, which he performed—date, April 29, 1745—in twelve hours, or at the rate of very nearly nineteen miles an hour. This is more than the speed of earliest so-called "*Parliamentary trains*".

It must be said, however, that Cooper Thornhill's rapid drive was regarded as something absolutely wonderful in his day. The road over which he passed on the memorable twenty-ninth of April, was lined' with spectators almost over its whole length, and the traveler was received with such enthusiastic cheers as if he had been a great king, or a man who had killed thousands— what people call a conqueror. A *mezzo-tinto* print of the famous exploit is still preserved, if I am not wrong, at hotel the Bell Inn at Stilton[23].

Coutts, at the period here sketched, stood by no means alone in being both bankers and corn-factors. *Fairholme of Edinburgh*, whose banking house had long been eminent, were also corn dealers on a large scale; and so were the firms of *Fordyce, Malcolm, and Co., Arbuthnot and Guthrie, Gibson and Hogg*, and many others. The only houses at Edinburgh, who confined themselves strictly to banking, were the two firms of *Mansfield and Co.*, and *William Cuming*. The founder of the first-named house, commonly called "old James Mansfield," began life in a very humble way, as a little draper in a back street, from which locality he emerged as a dealer in bills of exchange.

This led to more extended money transactions, ending in the establishment of a banking house of the first celebrity in Scotland. The firm of *Mansfield, Ramsay, and Co.*, continued to be of the highest eminence till 1807, when it merged its name into *Ramsays, Bonars, and Co.* In a similar manner the banking house of Cuming rose into existence. Old Patrick Cuming, that is, Cuming the first, kept a cloth shop in Parliament Close, which his son and heir, William, converted into a counting house, where he confined himself entirely to the trade in bills and money, with so

---

[23] History — The Bell Inn Hotel, Stilton, Peterborough, http://www.thebellstilton.co.uk/bell-inn-history

much success that after a long—probably also a hard —life, he died the possessor of a very considerable fortune. These individual examples show the difference in the origin of the leading English and the Scottish banking firms.

It was the failure of many of their corn and other businesses, which opened at last the eyes of the members of the firm of *Coutts and Co.*, to the value of banking, as the throughout most profitable of their commercial endeavours. The personal experience of James Coutts, the son of John, the hospitable Lord Provost, did much to accelerate the accomplishment of this model. James Coutts, who had never been out of Scotland, went on a visit to some friends in London, in August, 1754, and while here fell in love with a young damsel called Polly Peagrim, niece of *George Campbell*, banker in the Strand.

After a few weeks' courtship, Polly got wedded to James, and the event was followed by the entrance of the bridegroom into the firm of Campbell, henceforth called *Campbell and Coutts*. His London experience soon showed James Coutts that banking was better than corn dealing, even when taken in connection with smuggling tea and brandy, and he advised his friends in Scotland accordingly. Perhaps the advice would not have been so quickly taken, but for some simultaneous warnings in the shape of mercantile disasters.

The partners of the Scotch firm of *Coutts & Co.*, among whom was now Sir William Forbes and Mr. Hunter, the latter a very enterprising man, undertook various operations which they did not understand, with the consequence—to use an expressive colloquial phrase—to "*burn their fingers.*" They set up a large paper-mill at *Melville* with a substantial investment; but, when all was ready, discovered that they could not make paper, and had to consign their imperfect produce to America, from whence they learnt, through their agent, "*that the printers of the newspapers had bought some of the paper, because they could not find any of a better quality, and the apothecaries had bought the rest because they could not find any that was worse."* Not more fortunate than in paper-making were the partners in a lead-mine speculation.

They sunk gold, but got no lead in return; and though the phenomenon might have been explained, in a physical sense, by the fact that gold is much heavier than lead, and has consequently a much greater tendency to sink, the adventurers had but little comfort from it. But they took the wise resolution of keeping henceforward to banking, giving up all other businesses, even smuggling. This was about 1770; and the movement was followed *"by a number of other Scotch houses, previously devoted to trading speculations as well as banking."*

Probably, the number thus starting into existence, all at once, was too great, for after a little while there came a tremendous catastrophe. The disastrous event, as sudden as an earthquake, is still well remembered in Scotland, and generally spoken as *"the Black Monday"* — namely, Monday, the 8th of June, 1772. It will be necessary to return for a moment to London bankers and banking to understand the history of the Scotch *"Black Monday."*

# BLACK MONDAY

If, two hundred years ago, somebody had inquired at the Exchange, or the *Bank of England,* who was the most successful man of the day, the unfailing answer would have been, *"Alexander Fordyce."* His success in life, indeed, bordered on the marvelous; it was a sort of poetry of success—up to a certain time, for the prose followed soon after. There is much prose, unfortunately, at the bottom of all poetry, in life as well as in banking. Alexander Fordyce was bred a hosier, at Aberdeen; but finding this place too narrow for his abilities, he came to London, and after a short while succeeded in obtaining employment as an out-door clerk in the banking-house of *Boldero & Co.*

A handsome, dashing man, possessed of considerable energy of character, with a great flow of natural eloquence, and much suavity of manner, he soon attracted the attention not only of his masters, but of other gentlemen, and before long obtained an introduction to the family circle of *Roffey and Neale,* formerly brewers, and subsequently heads of the banking firm of *Roffey, Neale, and James*. At the private residence of these gentlemen, the young Aberdeen draper captivated all hearts, particularly the supposed soft ones of the fair sex; and the upshot of these conquests was, that Mr. Fordyce was offered a partnership in the banking-house of Roffey, Neale, and Co., in Threadneedle Street; which offer, it is needless to say, was accepted.

*Alexander Fordyce* had no sooner been thus comfortably established, when he began to trade in the public funds, hazarding large sums upon conjectural gains. Fortune, which is said to favour the bold—the proverb, like most proverbs, is of doubtful truth—smiled upon Alexander, showering the golden guineas into his lap by thousands and tens of thousands. His courage rose with his good luck, and his stakes doubled day after day. At last, in 1766, he had a great stroke of good luck in a speculation in East India Stock, He calculated upon a slight rise, and had no sooner invested his—that is his partners—fortune, when there took place an extraordinary upward movement, leaving him in the possession of profits amounting to near a hundred thousand pounds.

Alexander Fordyce now started fairly in the great race of life. He purchased a large estate, with splendid mansion, at *Roehampton*, and entered upon a series of feasts, banquets, and entertainments, which threw those of royalty in the shade. To show his zeal for religion, he built a church adjoining his mansion, supporting it by himself, and worshipping on a sort of velvet throne, surrounded by a glittering posse of tall footmen and bedizened lackeys. Alexander Fordyce next started as candidate for a seat in Parliament, which attempt, though he was not returned, cost him fourteen thousand pounds.

To secure his future election, he erected a hospital, and established other charities at the borough of his choice, leaving no means untried to become a senator, and openly avowing his hope to die a peer. As a beginning to this great end, he married a peeress, the *Lady Margaret Lindsay*, a daughter of the Earl of Balcarras, and sister of that Lady Anne Barnard whose name is so well-known as writer of "Auld Robin Gray." This was the highest stroke of good fortune that befell the handsome draper of Aberdeen.

Contemporary writers can scarcely find words to praise the beauty and grace of Lady Margaret "*Always sweet, always entertaining, always instructive,*" wrote Sheridan; while another added, "Her eloquence was remarkable, and her singing frequently left the whole room in tears." No wonder that, to please such a wife, as far above him by birth as by accomplishments, Alexander Fordyce redoubled speed in his wild career of extravagance. He purchased luxurious estates in Scotland, opened his mansion to the elite of rank and wealth, whom he entertained at sumptuous festivals, and grew insolent almost in the possession of his newly-acquired wealth. But the fatal period now approached when there came a turn in this tide of his success. Several speculations turned out badly, and his first losses brought a whole host of visible and invisible enemies against him. *"The stocks have got wind of this secret,"* said *Horace Walpole, "and their heart is fallen into their breeches—where the heart of the stocks is apt to lie."* Then came the affair of Falkland Island, which drove the funds down rapidly, leaving Fordyce, who had speculated on a rise, a loser to the extent of about a hundred thousand pounds.

To supply his deficiencies, he now had recourse to his partners' private funds. Discovery followed in the wake of this step, and the alarmed banker-brewers, as suddenly downcast as they had previously been elated, threatened exposure and punishment. *Roffey, Neale, and Co.,* had freely partaken of Fordyce's extreme good luck, and had rejoiced in the far ken which had attained them the services of so clever a person; but when they saw that the chances were going against him, they remonstrated with all the energy of men whose fortunes lay on the success of their remonstrances. Probably, they felt, with the "preternatural suspicion" of some of the heroes of the French Revolution, that the "Millennium was struggling on the threshold, and yet not so much as groceries could be had—owing to traitors." With what impetus will not men strike traitors in such a case.

Alexander Fordyce showed himself a great genius even in adversity. He treated the remonstrance of his partners with the most mortifying contempt, telling them that he was quite willing to leave a concern which they themselves were utterly incompetent to manage. At the same time, he showed them a thick pile of bank notes, which he had borrowed for the purpose; and the rustle of the bank notes, coupled with the magic of their insolent partner's eloquence, at once brought *Roffey & Neale* down upon their knees. But, although secure of the goodwill of his associates, the career of the young banker was fast drawing to a close. Getting desperate, he lost himself more and more in wild speculations, to cover which all his own and his friends resources were wholly insufficient. He next went about raising money by loans, but with very indifferent success.

The *Bank of England* refused support, and most of the private bankers declined too. Among those whom Alexander visited on his borrowing errand was a shrewd Quaker. *"Friend Fordyce,"* was the reply of the latter, *"I have known many men ruined by two dice, but I will not be ruined by Four-dice."* The Quaker was right, for a few days after, the collapse, which could now no longer be prevented, burst forth over the City.

Fordyce having absented himself from the banking-house in Threadneedle Street, his terrified partners, for the first time, investigated their accounts, and found they were forlornly bankrupt. The news created a panic; and the panic increased when it became known that the name of Alexander Fordyce was attached to bills in circulation to the amount of four million sterling. Such a Monday as this 8th day of June, 1772, had not been known in the commercial world of England within the memory of men, and people universally called it *"Black Monday."*

The *"Black Monday"* was a great calamity in England, but it proved almost fatal to the banking interest in Scotland. The news of the failure of Fordyce was brought to Edinburgh—according to the Scots Magazine of June, 1772 — "by a gentleman who posted from London in forty-three hours;" and it had the immediate effect of breaking nearly all the banks in the northern kingdom. The houses of *Douglas, Heron, & Co. (traded* as Ayr Bank)[24], *Arbuthnot & Guthrie, Andrew Sinclair & Co., Malcolm & Co., Johnston & Smith, William Alexander & Sons, Gibson & Balfour, Anthony Ferguson*, and many others, stopped payment one after another, and the panic at Edinburgh and Glasgow was such as to threaten an insurrection.

Besides the *Bank of Scotland, Royal Bank*, and *British Linen Company*, which were established by public authority, the only private banks that remained solvent were *Coutts & Co.*, and the houses of the two old drapers, Mansfield and Cuming. Coutts' firm was partly saved by the opportune arrival of a partner with a small sum in cash only between 2,000ʃ to 3,000ʃ —which common report, as usual, magnified into a couple of millions. In consequence, the people clamored for their money at other banks, where it would have been perfectly safe, to carry it to the second floor of the old house in Parliament Close with the imaginary million.

The most important effect of *"Black Monday"* in Scotland, was that it destroyed the *first joint-stock bank*, and thus prevented the growth of joint-stock enterprise for significant time—killing the flower in the bud. A banking firm, trading similar to the style of *Douglas, Heron, & Co.*, having its headquarters at *Ayr*, had been set up, in 1769, with a capital of 96,000ʃ, subscribed by about one hundred and forty shareholders.

The bank was managed for a time with considerable talent; but the directors committed at the outset the serious blunder of issuing a larger number of notes than was warranted by their subscribed capital, on the supposition that the number

---

[24] The Burns Encyclopedia.
http://www.robertburns.org/encyclopedia/DouglasHeronampCompan y.294.shtml

of partners—all liable, not "limited," but with their whole fortune— would form the best guarantee of their commercial transactions. But this expectation was doomed to disappointment.

"Black Monday" caused a run upon *Douglas, Heron, & Co.*, as well as all the other banks; the excited multitude claiming cash in exchange for their notes, regardless of the well-known fact that one hundred and forty gentlemen, some of them among the wealthiest landowners in Scotland, were responsible for every note issued by the bank.

There existed, however, a human stampede, not to be halted by any amount of sound sense and reasoning, and the consequence was that the new joint-stock bank had to declare itself insolvent. It was in vain that leading shareholders of the highest rank, such as the *Duke of Buccleuch* and the *Duke of Queensberry*, went to the *Bank of England* to seek assistance; they were told that the bank held already *Douglas, Heron, & Co.*'s notes to the amount of £150,000, and was indisposed to trust them any further.

The fact that the *Bank of England,* formed on joint-stock principles, was jealous of rival joint-stock enterprise, was well known in Scotland, and caused a loud burst of indignation from the shareholders of the unfortunate bank; but did not prevent its fall. The firm of *Douglas, Heron, & Co.,* closed business at the end of the third year, leaving, in the words of a Scotch writer, "*an amount of destruction in its wake such as Scotland had not experienced since the wreck of the Darien expedition.*"

It is said that a large portion of the land of the county of Ayr changed hands in consequence. For the remainder of their lives, the unfortunate shareholders in the *Ayr bank* had never done with paying; and in some instances, the descendants of shareholders did not get their accounts closed till sometime after the passing of the Reform Act, at the distance of upwards of sixty years from *"Black Monday."*

## SCOTCH JOINT-STOCK BANKS

The oldest joint-stock bank in the United Kingdom, the *Bank of England*, was established by a Scotchman; but while nearly a century and a half elapsed here before the example thus set was followed on a large scale, the seed took early root and flourished in Scotland in all directions. The earliest notice of banking in Scotland which occurs in the statute-book, is an act of King William the Third, passed in 1695, under which the Bank of Scotland was established. By this act, an exclusive privilege of banking was conferred for a limited time upon the Bank, it being provided, *"that for the period of twenty years, from the 17th July, 1695, it shall not be lawful for any other person to set up a distinct company or bank within the kingdom of Scotland, besides those persons in whose favour this act is granted."*

However, while the privilege of the *Bank of England* was renewed from time to time, no renewal took place in the case of the *Bank of Scotland*, and private enterprise in the latter country remained free and unfettered. It was partly this, and partly the cautious economical habits of the people in the north, which brought banking into far more extensive use, particularly among the lower classes of the population.

The establishment of the *Bank of Scotland* was followed, in 1727, by that of the *Royal Bank*; in 1746 by the *British Linen Company*; in 1763, by the *Dundee Banking Company*; and in 1766, by the *Perth Banking Company*. All these joint-stock banks differed in many important points from the early private banks and the one great public *Bank of England*. All the *Scotch banks issued small notes; all of them granted interest on the balance of current accounts*; all of them made advances to the public by way of *"cash credit;"* and nearly *all of them had branches*, which extended their usefulness into the remotest parts of the country.

The *Bank of Scotland* began to issue one-pound notes as early as 1704, and most of the other banks followed the example, there being no restriction whatever upon the issue of promissory notes, payable to the bearer on demand, for a sum of not less than twenty shillings. In England, the issue of notes for a less sum than five pounds, was prohibited by law from 1777. More important in its effects than this issue of small notes, was the early *system adopted by the Scotch banks of granting interest on the balance of current accounts*, and, at the same time, *taking deposits of a very small amount*.

Thus, while the bankers of England were—and still are to the present day—the purse-keepers of the rich, like their predecessors, the ancient goldsmiths, the *bankers of Scotland started on an entirely new plan by making themselves the trustees of the savings of the poor*. Some curious evidence, illustrating this notable point in the history of Scotch banking, was given before a committee of the House of Lords which sat in 1826. A witness who had been connected for many years with different banks in Scotland, and had gathered experience on the subject at Aberdeen, Edinburgh, Glasgow, Perth, and Stirling, stated that *more than one-half of the deposits in the banks which he had known were in sums of from ten to two hundred pounds*.

Being asked from what classes of the community the depositors came, he replied: "*They are generally the labouring classes in towns like Glasgow; but in country places, like Perth and Aberdeen, the deposits come from servants and fishermen, and that class of the community who save small sums from their earnings.*" This statement is worth noting mainly for those who are opposing the idea of *crowd funding*; but still more so the following, made by the same witness before the House of Lords, and which, as it explains Scotch banking, also shows the great influence it has exercised on the social life of the northern kingdom. "*Half-yearly, or yearly,*" so goes the statement, *"these depositors (laborers, servants, and fishermen) come to the bank, and add the savings of their labour, with the interest that has accrued upon the deposits, to the principal; and in this way it runs on accumulating at compound interest, till the depositor is able either to buy or build a house, when it comes to be one, or two, or three hundred pounds; or till he is able to commence business as a master in the line in which he has hitherto been a servant. A great part of the depositors of our banks are of that description, and the great part of the most thriving of our farmers and manufacturers have arisen from such beginnings."*

It is very strange that in England this extended system of banking, embracing the lower as well as the upper classes, should never have come into operation, although its effects are clearly beneficial to the banking interest, as well as to the industrial habits of the people. Even at present the practice of saving, so far from being encouraged among the British, is almost prohibited. It is not only that English bankers scorn to burden themselves with the small earnings of *"laborers, servants, and fishermen,"* but that the Government itself, which has long intruded in banking, as it has recently encroached upon life-insurance— playing the Napoleonic part of Patent-happiness-distributor — has actually made saving penal.

During early nineteenth century, no one was allowed to save more than £150 or, with accumulated interest, £200; and, should the industrial propensities go further, and the thrifty creature invest his or her money in a second Government institution, misnamed a *savings-bank*, the sum so invested is liable to forfeit and confiscation. To parody the words of the Scotch witness before the House of Lords, it may be said that *"a great part of the most thriving of our farmers and manufacturers have not arisen from such beginnings."*

The growth and development of joint-stock banking in Scotland was accelerated by a practice little known in England, namely, the mode of making advances by way of *"cash credit."* The system is well described in the report of the Lords' Committee on Scotch Banking of 1826. *"There is also,"* the report says, *" one part of their system, which is stated by all the witnesses—and, in the opinion of the committee, very justly stated—to have had the best effects upon the people of Scotland, and particularly upon the middle and poorer classes of society, in producing and encouraging habits of frugality and industry. The practice referred to is that of 'cash credits.' Any person who applies to a bank for a cash credit is called upon to produce two or more competent sureties, who are jointly bound; and after a full inquiry into the character of the applicant, the nature of his business, and the sufficiency of his securities, he is allowed to open a credit, and to draw upon the bank for the whole of its amount, or for such part as his daily transactions may require. To the credit of the account, he pays in such sums as he may not have occasion to use, and interest is charged or credited upon the daily balance, as the case may be. From the facility which these cash credits give to all the small transactions of the country, and from the opportunities which they afford to persons who begin business with little or no capital but their character, to employ profitably the minutest products of their industry, it cannot be doubted that the most important advantages are derived to the whole community. The advantage to the banks who give these cash credits arises from the call which they continually produce for the issue of the paper, and from the opportunity which they afford for the profitable employment of part of their deposits. The banks are, indeed, so sensible of it, that, in order to make this part of their business advantageous and secure, they hold it necessary that their cash credits should, as they express it, be frequently operated upon, and they refuse to continue them unless this implied condition be fulfilled. The total amount of their cash credits is stated by one witness to be five millions."* The system undoubtedly was of considerable influence in the early establishment of *joint-stock banking in Scotland.*

It must be stated, however, that there was another circumstance connected with Scotch legislation which much accelerated the growth of northern joint-stock enterprise, while, not existing in England, it could not operate in the same manner here. The law of Scotland tended greatly to place the mutual relations of bankers and their clients upon a secure footing, both by affording ready means for attaching a debtor's property, whether consisting in land or movables, and by giving unusual facilities for ascertaining the financial conditions of men possessed of real estate, the class from which come most of the shareholders of the old—not "limited"—joint-stock banks.

A creditor in Scotland is permitted to attach the real and transmissible as well as the personal estate of his debtor for payment of personal debts, among which are categorized debts due by bills and promissory notes; and option may be had, for the purpose of securing payment, to each account of property at the same time. Execution, likewise, is not confined to the real property of a debtor during his lifetime, but proceeds with equal effect after his death.

The law for the formation of records gives, moreover, ready means of securing information with respect to the real and transmissible estate of which any person in Scotland may be controlled. No purchase of an estate is valid until the "*seisine,*" the document certifying that actual delivery has been given, is put on record; nor is any mortgage effective until the deed is in like manner recorded. These records are accessible to all persons, and thus the public can with ease ascertain the effective means which a banking company possessor of discharging its obligations[25]; while the managers of banks are allowed to decide, with acceptable precision, the degree of risk and obligation which they incur in their transactions. It was on this basis— within a ring-fence pretty well secured by property laws forged by the iron hands of the ancient Romans—that there sprang into existence the *Scotch society of joint-stock banking*.

It took many years, almost a century, before England followed in the same direction. The struggle to establish joint-stock banking in England was long and severe—one of the severest commercial battles fought in the history of finance.

---

[25] Similar to the modern concept of Blockchain, in which a Public ledger is maintained and accessible to everybody.

# BANKING MONOPOLY

Adam Smith, in his "Wealth of Nations," truly remarks that, *"Though the principles of the banking trade may appear somewhat abstruse, the practice is capable of being reduced to strict rules. To depart upon any occasion from these rules, in consequence of some flattering speculation of extraordinary gain, is almost always dangerous, and frequently fatal to the banking company which attempts it. But the constitution of joint-stock companies renders them in general more tenacious of established rules than any private co-partnership. Such companies, therefore, seem extremely fitted for this trade."*

Sir Henry Parnell gives his testimony to the same effect: *"The trade of banking,"* says he, *"is of such a nature that it is scarcely possible for any but a very numerous body of partners to furnish a capital sufficiently large for carrying it on advantageously to the public. A single individual or a few individuals cannot be, but very rarely, possessed of that amount of capital which alone can render this trade a safe one; for this reason, in order to establish in a country a sound system of banking, it is indispensably necessary that care should be taken not to impose any legislative restrictions in the way of large bodies associating together to form joint-stock banking companies."*

It seems astonishing that, with such authorities in favour of a principle, clearly and generally recognised, it should have taken above a century to establish joint-stock banking in England. The fact appears strange; but the cause lies on the surface. It was simply the monopoly, real or assumed, of the first joint-stock bank which barred other banks on the same principle from being established. *William Paterson*, the founder of the *Bank of England*, by no means intended to create a monopoly in favour of his own system when he introduced the principle of joint-stock banking into this country; but by a curious agreement of circumstances, the very organization which was invented by the shrewd Scot, himself an opponent of all monopolies, to encourage and foster the trade in money, ultimately served to hamper and obstruct it for generations to come.

From the beginning, the *Bank of England* was opposed by some of the leading members of the commercial community in the City, who argued that *"it would become a monopoly, and engross the whole money of the kingdom; and that, as it must infallibly be subservient to Government views, it might be applied to the worst purposes of arbitrary power."* Against these claims the Bank defended itself, in a pamphlet from the pen of Michael Godfrey, already cited. The writer disclaimed the idea that the Bank desired to have a monopoly, asserting that the monopolizing tendencies were all on the part of the enemies of the new institution.

*"The goldsmiths,"* he said, *"have been guilty of engrossing most commodities themselves, and they have also been great merchants and traders. And since the nation has suffered so much by their monopolising goods and trading with other men's stocks, it may seem highly reasonable that, as the Bank is restrained from trade, for fear of those mischiefs which the goldsmiths have practised, so the goldsmiths, in like manner, should be limited to the selling plate and jewels, which was their ancient and proper trade."*

In the latter sentence prowled the treacherous part of the spirit which guided the administrators of the great public bank. The desire to restrain and to limit the activity of others, in order to have greater room for activity themselves, soon carried the directors of the Bank of England from passive to aggressive measures, driving them, as a consequence, more and more under the shield and protection of the Government.

At the same time, *William Paterson*, who did not sympathize with these proceedings, was ousted from his post as governor, without the least recognition of his distinguished services. Moving onward in this direction, it gradually came to pass that a joint-stock society, originally consisting of 1,300 persons, with no other purpose in view than that of getting a fair interest for a subscribed capital of little more than a million, was transformed into a huge official corporation. This led to a struggle, extending over a century, between private enterprise, on the one hand, and vested interests assuming the form of monopoly, on the other.

By the original charter of the Bank of England its privileges were very limited, interposing no obstacle to the establishment of other joint-stock banking companies, either of issue or deposit. In significance, the early success of the Bank brought forth several projects of the same kind—unfortunately very hollow in substance, and deeply tinged with the swindling element. The two greatest of these schemes, which had, in their sad consequences, the worst effects upon the character of the infant Joint-stock, were the *"Land Bank,"* projected by *Dr. Hugh Chamberlain*, and the *"Charitable Corporation Fund,"* got up by several Members of Parliament, chief among them *Sir Archibald Grant* and *Sir Robert Sutton*.

The Land Bank —*"the romantic Land Bank"* as some pamphleteers (*peers of modern day bloggers*) of the day called it—was established for the purpose of advancing money upon landed property: a project taken up by French a century and a-half later in their *Credit Fancier*, The system seems to have succeeded pretty well in the beginning, for, we are told, that "estates to a very great value were subscribed for in a short space, a deed settled, a company formed, and all things disposed to put the matter into execution." However, although the number of people willing to mortgage their freeholds was large enough, the money to be lent was slow in forthcoming, and so the bank failed. Its existence was marked principally by a paper war with the Directors of the Bank of England, in which it was held that the latter got the worst. One fly-sheet, of 1696, proclaims "the trial and condemnation of the Land Bank at Exeter Change, for Murdering the Bank of England at Grocers' Hall;" while another gives as epitaph, "Here lies the body of the Bank of England, who was born in 1694, and died May 5, 1696, in the third year of its age."

The jocularity of the *Land Bank* was harmless; less so were the doings of the *Charitable Corporation Fund*. It was started in 1705, with the avowed object of encouraging commerce and industry by taking money on deposit from the upper as well as the middle and lower classes of society, making it a sort of *savings bank*, and lending the funds thus obtained to small traders and manufacturers, somewhat after the manner of the *cash-credit system* in use in Scotland.

The new joint-stock bank was very successful in the first few years of its existence, so much so that the directors felt warranted in increasing the original capital of the company by £60,000[26]. The money was immediately contributed, and there

---

[26] In 2017, the relative value of £60,000 from 1705 ranges from £8,644,000 to £1,173,000,000. For detailed analysis, see https://www.measuringworth.com/ukcompare/relativevalue.php?use %5B%5D=CPI&use%5B%5D=NOMINALEARN&year_early=1705&pound

was a perfect enthusiasm on the part of many people with "*limited incomes*," such as clergymen, widows, and others, to invest their savings in the Charitable Corporation Fund.

This eagerness, however, was suddenly stopped by a rumour that the affairs of the society were in a chaotic state followed by the fatal news that the company was bankrupt. Crowds at the door; a wild outcry for money, and cries in the newspapers followed, as a matter of course; after which came an official declaration of bankruptcy. Investigation proved the history of the bank a very sad one. The directors had borrowed, or simply taken, large sums on fictitious pledges: they had falsified the books, corrupted the servants of the company, and cheated the depositors. About half a million sterling had disappeared in this way, leading to the ruin of vast numbers of people.

The suffering caused by this catastrophe is described in contemporary accounts as terrible, and far beyond what the breaking of any bank in the kingdom would occasion at the present day. It is stated in one or two papers, though it seems barely credible, that the loss of their whole fortune drove some women of rank and character to sell themselves in exchange for bread. Parliament, decently shocked by all these horrors, and urged on by the outcry of a crowd of ill-fated depositors, instigated what was called a strict inquiry; but it led to nothing.

The *Jacobites*, too, tried to make political capital out of the disaster by laying hands on one of the swindlers of the bank who had fled to Rome, and announcing, in a letter addressed to

---------------------------------

71=60000&shilling71=&pence71=&amount=60000&year_source=170 5&year_result=2017

the House of Commons, that *"James the Third,"* in other words, the Pretender, was ready to give up the criminal from the castle of St. Angelo, where he was held a prisoner. In reply, the House voted that the letter from James the Third should be burned at the Royal Exchange by the common hangman. This was the last public notice of the Charitable Corporation Fund.

The poor, derelict depositors, it is to be supposed, soon got quiet, or died away, as ruined, ill-fated people are apt to do; and, when all was blown over, the clever and educated ne'er-do-wells returned from Italy and Switzerland, and bought estates in Middlesex. But though forgotten and forgiven, as all earthly things are, the tragic fate of the *Charitable Corporation Fund* exercised for a long time a depressing influence on the newborn faith in joint-stock companies.

It was, however, previous to the failure of the Corporation Fund that the Bank of England succeeded in obtaining a monopoly of joint-stock banking, or what was held to be such, from the Government. In 1708, the Bank, in addition to its other privileges, got an Act prohibiting the formation of any other banks with more than six partners, or, what amounted to the same, of any other joint-stock bank.

By a "little clause" inserted in the statute of the sixth of Anne, it was enacted *"that during the continuance of the governor and company of the Bank of England , it shall not be lawful for any body politic or corporate, united or to be united, other than the governor and company of the Bank of England , or for other persons whatsoever, united or to be united, in covenants or partnerships, exceeding the number of six persons, in this part of Great Britain called England, to borrow, owe, or take up, any sum or sums of money in their bills or notes payable on demand, or at any less time than six months from the borrowing thereof*." This clause acted as a bar to joint-stock banking in England for more than a century.

It took *one hundred and twenty years to notice* that the Act only prohibited the formation of joint-stock banks of issue, and had no effect upon banks of deposit. The fact that this should have been unnoticed for so long a time is one of the most singular illustrations of the tendency of mankind to take things upon trust, without inquiry and original analysis. An error, in its consequences of immense importance to the commercial classes of a country, was, in this instance, repeated from generation to generation, without any inconsistency whatever. The old saying that *men willingly believe what they wish to be true* was reversed on this notable occasion; for men, and shrewd business men too, actually took upon trust a fact which they neither wished nor hoped for, believing in the existence of a huge monopoly which the most apparent analysis would have been able to destroy.

# COUNTRY BANKING AND LOTTERIES

The passing of the Act of 1708 had the consequences expected by its supporters, the directors of the *Bank of England*. All co-partnerships of more than six persons being forbidden by law, several existing joint-stock banks had to wind up business, while projects of many new ones were killed in the bud. The Act tacitly gave encouragement to small shop-keepers, and people of fertile brains but limited means, to establish banks and issue notes, while it put a stop to the association of persons of position, respectability, and credit, willing to embark their capital in the same trade.

There was *no license required to set up as a banker*, nor was there, previous to 1774, *any legislative restriction to the issue of small notes*. Consequently, Lilliputian banking institutions sprang up, like mushrooms, all over England, as soon as the formidable competition of joint-stock banks was removed, and the trade was left to the great Government Bank on the one hand, and individual enterprise—often of the fraudulent kind— on the other.

It was in the provinces particularly that the business of banking remained, for the greater part of the eighteenth century, very little removed from that of the tailor or shoemaker. The origin of many of the more important country banks may even now be traced to these humble beginnings. The *"Old Gloucester Bank,"* was founded by a *James Wood*, in 1716, and was originally nothing but a chandler's shop of the smallest kind, the owner of which distinguished himself from other chandlers by discounting bills, as well as selling soap and cheese. The bank was continued by several generations of Woods, and though they made money fast, they did not give up the shop, but only enlarged it, and very likely sold their soap' at a better price.

*James Wood the Third*, a man notable as a Croesus in his days—he was born in 1756, and died in 1836—was the last to keep the ancestral shop, in which he sold almost everything, from a mouse-trap and a slice of baron to diamond bracelets and ducal coronets. The bacon-and-cheese business was conducted at one end of the shop, and at the other was the *Old Gloucester Bank*, which earls were not too proud to enter —knowing that the owner was worth a million. But the halo of his magic million did not make *James Wood the Third* a happy and contented man; on the contrary, he seems to have been, to the hour of his death, one of the most hard-worked and miserable creatures.

Swinging like a pendulum between his shop and his bank, the whole business of which he managed with two clerks, his existence was literally broken up by petty cares and anxieties. His dinner was settled to cost no more than four pence, and his sleep was regulated to be no more than six hours; while the remaining eighteen hours of morning, noon, and night, were spent in regular and unceasing vibrations between the two corners of counting-house and shop.

Of course, he was unmarried, the poor *banker-grocer*; and when he died, the great million which he had amassed fell into the lap of a score of cavernous relatives, all anxiously awaiting the decease of the old bachelor. However, though the fortune fell into their hands, the anxious *"friends"* did not get it after all. For between the cup and the lip there were still more eager heirs—priests of the blind goddess of justice, in Chancery Lane. Suits and cross suits, actions and counter actions, followed in the wake of the Probate of Will, and, at the hour that is, the gentlemen of the long robe must have well-nigh pocketed the million, gathered, with so much care and anxiety, in the old shop, by the three generations of *Woods of Gloucester*.

More illustrative still of the origin of many country banking houses than the foregoing example, is the rise of the old banking establishment of *Smith of Nottingham*, then merged in the well-known firm of *Smith, Payne, and Co.,* of Lombard-street. *Smith the First*, the Smith of all the other Smiths, was, at the beginning of the 18th century, a respectable draper at Nottingham, well frequented by the gudewives of the farmers, who bought their quarterly stock of thread and ribbons at his shop, after having sold their pigs. The wives, of course, brought the husbands, and though the latter wanted no caps and laces, they liked to have a quiet half hour in the cozy back parlour, to discuss the news of the day and the state of the markets with Smith.

A frequent theme of conversation was the danger of the roads. The neighbourhood of Nottingham, the home of *Robin Hood*, was, as ever, infested with footpads; and *Dick Turpin* himself, or one of the Dick Turpins, was believed to honour the country at times with his presence. It was not that the farmers feared for their wives, or their pigs; but they feared for their money, dearer to them than their pigs—it would be wrong to say their wives.

The bland draper, having long listened to these outpourings of woe, at last hit upon a ready solution of the difficulty. *"I will take care of your money,"* Smith proposed; *"and will, moreover, keep an account of your market transactions, and you may draw your cash, or get goods from me, whenever you like."* The offer was accepted, first by one, then by a dozen, then by a score of farmers; and soon Smith found himself the holder of very considerable sums of money. He was a shrewd man, the Nottingham draper; and the cash did not remain idle in his hands, as every man knew who had a good bill to discount anywhere in Notts or Lancashire.

The merchants of Preston themselves were often glad to get place, and the profits were as sure as the returns quick. Now

Smith took the second step in his flourishing career, and a very utilitarian one it was—he allowed a small interest to his friends the depositors. The pleased farmers, it need not be said, were, after this, perfectly enthusiastic in handing their surplus cash to the Nottingham draper, instead of putting it into an old stocking at home, where, whatever else might happen to it, it certainly would not grow. So, things went on in the natural course, until the draper became a regular banker, and, justly thinking his shop a hindrance to his business, gave up the trade in cloth and ribbons in favour of that in money and bills.

*Smith the First* died a Nottingham banker; and Smith the Second extended his-operations to Hull and Lincoln; while Smith the Third sought and found a London representative in the person of a shrewd and active man, Payne, with whom he subsequently entered into partnership. Hence the firm of *Smith, Payne, & Co.*, continued to flourished near the Mansion House, un-devoured by joint-stock. Later, as Royal Bank of Scotland's Heritage Hub notes[27]:

> During the eighteenth century, the London bank was seen as the parent bank, although the Smith family's country banks became more autonomous during the nineteenth century and eventually only three of the London partners held partnerships in the family's provincial banks. In 1837, new premises were built for Smith, Payne & Smiths in Lombard Street. The balance sheet in 1891 totalled £4.5 million. In 1899, when the combined balance sheets of the

---

[27] Smith, Payne & Smiths, RBS Heritage Hub, http://heritagearchives.rbs.com/companies/list/smith-payne-and-smiths.html

5 family banks amounted to over £10 million, the Lincoln bank's partners proposed amalgamation with Barclay & Co, leading to discussion of the future of the businesses amongst the Smith family banks. In 1902, the five Smith family banks, including Smith, Payne & Smiths, merged with Union Bank of London Ltd of London, to form Union of London & Smiths Bank Ltd.

It was the policy of the *Bank of England*, while resisting the establishment of joint-stock undertakings, to favour as much as possible the growth of private banks throughout the country; and this had the effect of giving, in a comparatively short space of time, a bank, or what passed as such, to almost every town in the kingdom. Unfortunately, many of these bankers were not of the strictly respectable class, and, to make money, did not scruple to mix themselves up with all sorts of, if not illegal, at least immoral pursuits. One of the worst of these, and which, although supported by Government, led to endless crime and misery, was the LOTTERY SYSTEM.

Lotteries, like banking, came from Italy to England, and it is probable that the identical *"Longobards"* who set up their stalls on the *"messuage sometime belonging to Robert Turke, abutting on Lombard Street toward the south, and toward Comhill on the north,"* were selling foreign lottery tickets as well as exchanging foreign coin. Certain it is that lotteries of various kinds originated at a very early time in Italy. They were taken under the protection of the State, as a means of filling the public exchequer, at Genoa, towards the end of the fourteenth century. The Papal Government, always in want of cash, quickly followed the example— continued, with not praiseworthy conservatism, to the present day—of alluring people into games of hazard; and fostered by the Holy Mother Church, as well as encouraged by priests and merchants, by Jews and Lombards, the passion of lotteries soon spread all over Europe. The infection at last was carried into the islands.

Urged on by her astute advisers, Queen Elizabeth consented to the introduction of the pernicious system into her dominions. The first proposals for a *"national lottery"* were published in the autumn of 1568, and so great was the eagerness of the people to participate in the expected golden harvest, that the whole of the forty-thousand *"chances,"* at ten shillings each—a very considerable amount in those days—were sold in a couple of months, and many of the tickets were disposed of at a premium.

The drawing commenced on the 11th of January, 1569, at the west door of *St Paul's Cathedral*, and lasted, day and night, without interruption, till the 6th of May following, amidst a boundless excitement of the people. It was in vain that stern moralists lifted their voices against the evil, at the risk of being stoned for lack of patriotism—on the appeal that the net proceeds of the lottery were destined for the repairs of the harbour and havens of the English coast.

However, though the thing was successful. Queen Elizabeth was not delighted with the new mode of raising money, and during her rule there were no more national lotteries. King James was less scrupulous, and in the same year that he created baronets *"for the raising of money to colonize Ulster,"* he reintroduced public lotteries, *"for the benefit of the Virginia colonies."* A London tailor, whose name history has not handed down to us, gained the first prize of 4,000 crowns, which caused such an excitement among the lower classes of the London population, as to make them invest their last penny in lotteries.

The licentious consequences were so inordinate that, after a few more public drawings, they were suspended by an Order in Council of March, 1620. *Charles I* at the start of his reign, rejuvenated lotteries, under the pretense of collecting funds for a project of conveying water to London; and though Parliament verboten the system soon after, *it crept up again among the people in a thousand different forms*.

In 1694, there was another great State lottery, which put a million into the exchequer of *William III*; and, for the next century, gambling, sanctioned by the Government, thrived as it had never before in England. Many of the small country bankers made a fortune as lottery agents, and even metropolitan houses of high standing were not above accepting "chances" as a security for loans. The mania rose to the wildest pitch during the latter part of the eighteenth century, when the example set by Government was followed, to an unmeasured extent, by all classes of the population.

In 1772, there were lottery tailors, lottery hatters, lottery staymakers, lottery tea-merchants, lottery barbers—offering a shave and the expectation of winning £10 in exchange for a three-penny ticket—lottery shoeblacks, lottery eating-houses— where a fellow had a chance of getting a meal and fifty pounds for six pence— lottery oyster stalls, with a dozen live "natives," and a remote prospect of five guineas—and a hundred similar institutions.

The lottery-men, careless of the dreadful devastation they were spreading through the length and breadth of the land, were quite corrupt as regards the means employed in fostering their nefarious schemes. *Clergymen were enlisted to advocate gambling as a patriotic duty*; the *Bible was ransacked to prove the antiquity and sanctity of lotteries*; and influential merchants and bankers were induced to put their names to lottery schemes of the greatest effrontery. The willingness of not a few heads of banking establishments to engage in these speculations is shown by the fact that, *in 1751, no less than 30,000 lottery-tickets were accepted in pawn by the metropolitan bankers*. For a time *"chances"* became an established security in Lombard Street, side by side with bills of exchange and *Bank of England* notes.

The Bank authorities themselves were mixed up, more or less, with the lottery system, while under the patronage of Mr. Vansittart, Chancellor of the Exchequer. The proposed inscription over his tomb forms an epitomized history of the period: — *"Here lies the Right Honourable Nicholas Vansittart, once Chancellor of the Exchequer, who patronised Bible Societies, built churches, encouraged savings banks, and supported lotteries."*

# THE BATTLE OF JOINT-STOCK

The political and financial crisis of 1793 showed in conspicuous light the impish effects of the legislation of that day, which, by preventing the establishment of joint-stock banks, encouraged the growth of plentiful small tradesmen in the country passing by the name of bankers but undeserving the title. One of the causes, and by no means the least important, of the disaster was to be found in the reckless operations of many of these local banks, particularly their unchecked issue of notes. There were at this period about *three hundred country bankers who manufactured paper money, some of them very liberally; and more than 'two hundred of them issued what were termed "optional notes," payable either in the metropolis or in the country.*

These little bits of paper, often mere rags, and in nearly all instances but pictorial representations of funds which did not exist, came floating up to London in great amounts, very undesirable in the shops, yet taken on the credit of the carriers. Much intrigue was resorted to on the part of the country bankers to push their paper into the great circle of trade; the member for the borough seldom came up to St. Stephen's without having his pocket-book stuffed with the-notes of some unknown firm of grocers or haberdashers, and his wife invariably made it a point to settle metropolitan millinery and dressmakers bills in paper money of native growth.

Of course, when the disaster came, the "optional notes" were found to be little better than waste paper, and a cry of distress went through the land *when a couple of hundred country bankers all at once suspended payment*[28].

The shock was so ferocious as to upset the great protecting bank together with the little protected ones. On the 8th of October, 1795, the directors of the *Bank of England* sent a first message to the Chancellor of the Exchequer claiming assistance in their need. No notice was taken of this communiqué, nor of subsequent pleas, which came more and more persistent in the spring and summer of 1796. Finally, on the 9th of February, 1797, the Court of Directors ordered the Governor of the Bank to tell Mr. Pitt that the long-threatening collapse was fast approaching.

This last call for support took effect. On the 26th February, a meeting of the Privy Council was held, in which it was resolved "that the Directors of the Bank should forbear issuing any cash." This order was followed by a notice of the Directors, stating that they were restrained from doing what, in fact, was absolutely impossible for them to do, namely, to give cash for their paper. They added, nevertheless, that *"the general concerns of the bank were in the most affluent condition."* The statement was received for what it was worth; and the general impression upon the public caused by the bankruptcy of the Government establishment was shown in an exceptional fall in public funds as well as in the stock of the *Bank of England*.

---

[28] Here I am pointing towards the fact that in a matter not more than of a few months, 833 digital currencies had sprung out in early 2017, many of them without solid value behind them, being speculated for $31,410,729,018 on the 26th of April, 2017.

The distress of the Government establishment gave new courage to the friends of joint-stock banking, and fresh attempts were made to upset the monopoly of the *Bank of England*. On the 30th May, 1797, *Sir William Pulteney* submitted to the House of Commons a bill *"for the erection of a new bank in case the Bank of England did not pay in specie on or before the 24th of June, 1797."* He entered into a detailed history of the Bank, pointing out the injury produced by monopoly, and proposing that it was nothing but a premium for lethargy and negligence, and productive of endless malice to the trade and commerce of the country. He enumerated a variety of facts to convince the House that the Bank had lost its charter by violating its engagements with the public.

Mr. Sheridan, who followed, said, *"he considered it a farce to call that a bank whose promise to pay on demand was paid by another promise to pay at some undefined period. It was ridiculous to think of placing confidence in paper, upon any principle but that of its being paid when it became due."* The speech made some impression; but all chance of the success of *Sir William Pulteney's bill* vanished when Mr. Pitt rose, and declared in strong terms in favour of the Bank monopoly. The bill was lost; but the struggle was renewed in the House of Commons in less than three years after. To calm the storm, the Bank had choice this time to a dogged act of bribery.

At a general meeting of the proprietors of bank stock, held on the 9th January, 1800, it was resolved that the Bank should make an offer to the Government to advance, *without interest*, the sum of three million sterling, on the security of Exchequer Bills payable on the 5th of April, 1806. Parliament accepted the enticement, and in consideration thereof extended the company's privileges —prohibiting all partnerships of more than six persons from banking operations in England— from the 1st of August, 1813, the time at which the monopoly would otherwise have expired, till the 1st of August, 1833. Thus, by a judicious expenditure of a fraction of their enormous profits, the shareholders of the one joint-stock bank had their interests secured for another generation.

The battle against the *Bank of England* was renewed sufficiently early to prevent a fresh grant of monopoly at the expiration of this charter. In the session of 1825-6 a bill was sanctioned by the lower *House of Parliament*, permitting co-partnerships for banking purposes throughout England *"except in London and within a distance of sixty-five miles thereof."* On the 17th of February, 1826, this bill was brought under the notice of the House of Lords, and gave rise to a notable speech by the Prime Minister, the *Earl of Liverpool*: — *"The present system of law as to banks,"* he exclaimed, *"must now be altered, in one way or another. It is the most absurd, the most inefficient legislation; it has not one recommendation to stand upon. The present system is one of the fullest liberty as to what is rotten and bad; but of the most complete restriction as to all that is good. By it a cobbler, or a cheese monger, may issue his notes, without any proof of his ability to meet them, and unrestricted by any check whatever; while, on the other hand, more than six persons, however respectable, are not permitted to become partners in a bank with whose notes the whole business of the country might be transacted. Altogether, the whole system is so absurd, both in theory and practice that it would not appear to deserve the slightest support if it was attentively considered even for a single moment."*

Notwithstanding this very outspoken declaration. Lord Liverpool did not go far in his support of joint-stock banking, but contented himself in passing the new bill, which left to *"cobblers and cheesemongers"* their full banking privileges, and kept the ground for sixty-five miles around the metropolis as a rich preserve to the *Bank of England.* Meanwhile, however, another movement came to be developed, which isolated from the Bank its old friends and *protégés* —the country bankers. On the 26th of May, 1826, an Act was passed for making it lawful for the directors of the *Bank of England "to authorise and empower any committee or committees, agent or agents, to carry on the business of banking,"* in other words, to establish branch banks.

The country bankers thereupon flew to arms, and on the 7th of December, 1827, a meeting of delegates of the body was held in London, when, after a due number of fierce speeches, a resolution was come to condemning branches of the *Bank of England* , and, indeed all other banking establishments, save the existing ones, which, it was asserted, were *"intimately-connected with the prosperity of trade, the support of agriculture, the increase of general improvement, and the productiveness of the national revenue."*

But it was in vain that Government was assaulted by deputations, and *Bank of England* directors threatened with the anger of the country magnates. His Majesty's advisers, in reply to numerous addresses, merely promised the stereotyped "due attention," while the governors of the Bank, having now to fight two enemies, preferred incurring the displeasure of half a thousand country bankers to neglecting the opposition of the rising giant, Joint-stock. Heedless of the cries and wailings of their old friends, the directors of the *Bank of England* at once opened a number of branches—at Gloucester, Manchester, and Swansea, in 1826; at Birmingham, Liverpool, Bristol and Leeds, in 1827; and at Newcastle in 1828.

Lancashire and Yorkshire took the lead in profiting by the Act of 1826, which permitted the establishment of joint-stock banks beyond the radius of sixty-five miles from London. The

*"Lancashire Banking Company,"* with 127 partners, was founded on the 9th of October, 1826, and its immediate success prompted the establishment of the *"Huddersfield Banking Company,"* with 335 partners, on the 7th June, 1827. In both cases the shareholders numbered among them the wealthiest and most influential men of the district, mostly from the merchant and manufacturing classes. The same year, 1827, saw two other joint-stock banks established, at Bradford and at Carlisle, the former with 173, and the latter with 19 shareholders. It is curious to note the gradual but secure rise in public favour of these first English joint-stock banks.

The *Lancashire Banking Company*, the pioneer of the coming host, was established with a nominal capital of only £300,000, divided in 3,000 shares, and paid a dividend of 5 percent, during the first few years, which then rose to seven and half percent, and in 1835 to 10 percent. The *Huddersfield Banking Company*, with a nominal capital of £700,000—but only £65,000 paid up —gave its shareholders a 6 percent, dividend for four years, and nineteen percent, in 1833. The *Bradford joint-stock bank* began with seven and half percent, and after two years' existence returned 10 percent, interest on the capital; and at a similar rate were the dividends of other banking companies, founded within the next few years in the provinces.

That the capitalists of London should be prohibited from embarking in these profitable undertakings, while trade in the country was free, seemed an anomaly too atrocious to be borne; and accordingly, strong efforts were made in 1830, and during the following years, to get a repeal of the sixty-five miles' clause. Pending these efforts, a daring joint-stock speculator discovered a shorter road to the goal of his desires. He made the extraordinary discovery that the dreaded statutes, made to guard the monopoly of the *Bank of England* as with walls of granite, were the merest cobwebs. *"You can drive in a carriage and four through any Act of Parliament*," says the proverb. The fact was once more proved by a man of very remarkable talents, a first-rate "driver," James William Gilbert, founder of the London and Westminster Bank.

# THE LONDON AND WESTMINSTER BANK

Since joint-stock banks have come to pay 20 percent, to their shareholders the faith in them has been limitless, and few realize the colossal difficulty which there was, only thirty years ago, to start such activities, even in the British metropolis. It has been with joint-stock banks as with railways—they had at first but few helpers and many foes, and the need of quantities had to be made up by high resolve and fearless autonomy on the part of the leaders. One of these leaders was *James William Gilbart*, the creator of the *London and Westminster Bank*. He commenced his career in 1813, as junior clerk to a London banker, and remained in this position for twelve years. At the end of the period he was appointed manager of the Kilkenny branch of the *Provincial Bank of Ireland*; but returned to London in 1833 to assist in establishing one or more joint-stock banks, in the teeth of the monopoly of the *Bank of England*.

While reform associations had run their engines against Parliament to induce it to rescind the clause in the Charter of the *Bank of England* , barring the formation of any bank with more than six partners ; while pamphlets immeasurable were hurled against the Act, and the important lawyers of Great Britain were fighting *pro* and *contra,* Gilbart quietly stepped forward and declared that there was no Act of Parliament in existence forbidding the creation of joint-stock banks of deposit in London, or anywhere else in the British dominions. When the statement was first made, some laughed, some got angry, and some called the innovators bad names—the three approved modes of opposing anything new that is said or done in the world.

However, Gilbart and his friends continued in their proclamations, and, to show their seriousness, at once began the formation of a joint-stock bank on a large scale in the metropolis. Of course, the directors of the *Bank of England* rushed to arms;

but, to their infinite surprise, discovered that their title-deeds indeed were as bad as was proclaimed. The teachers of statute law, having once more put on their best spectacles, now declared that the new bank promoters were quite right, and that all the world had been quite wrong for the last hundred and twenty years; that, in fact, the *Bank of England* held no monopoly, or, at the best, but the fraction of one, regarding joint-stock banks of issue.

So also, ruled the Solicitor-General, consulted on the part of the Government. He maintained, in decided terms, that the establishment of joint-banks of deposit was not an encroachment on the privileges of the *Bank of England,* there being no Act of Parliament, or any other law whatever, to prohibit such partnerships. The declaration fell like a thunderbolt on the friends of the Old Lady in Threadneedle Street. They protested, of course; but what can protests affect against "legal opinions," backed by formidable law officers of the Crown? What was the worst being that the world did not sympathize with the sufferings of the Old Lady, but seemed rather inclined to take the part of her opponents.

When at length fair progress had been made in the attempt to establish a joint-stock bank in London, Government bethought itself of welcoming the arrival of the little stranger, and sanctioning its existence in a proper legal manner. Accordingly, an Act was brought in— 3rd and 4th William IV. cap. 98—annulling the "*construction*" put by the public upon former Acts, and embodying the most recent legal wisdom.

The new Act ran as follows:—"*And whereas doubts have arisen as to the construction of the said Acts, and as to the extent of such exclusive privilege [of the Bank of England ], and it is expedient that all such doubts should be removed: be it therefore declared and enacted, That anybody, politic or corporate, or society, or company, or partnership, although consisting of more than six persons, may carry on the trade or business of banking in London, or within sixty-five miles thereof, provided that such body, politic or corporate, or society, or company, or partnership, do not borrow, owe, or take up in England any sum or sums of money on their bills or notes payable on demand, or at any less time than six months from the borrowing thereof, during the continuance of the privileges granted to the said governor and company of the Bank of England ."*

Immediately after the passing of this Act, in May, 1833, a final prospectus was issued for the formation of the London and Westminster Bank. It met with much secret, as well as open opposition on the part of the private bankers and others interested in the existing state of things, and the consequence was that the shares of the new bank could be disposed of but with the greatest difficulty. However, the organizers were thoroughly in earnest. Seeing that people in town would not take the shares, they went into the country, and, by dint of immense efforts, succeeded in getting a paid-up capital of £50,000 with which very moderate sum they determined to make their start in the world. On this foundation, the *London and Westminster Bank commenced business in Throgmorton Street, on the 10th of March, 1834.*

Thus, far the battle of joint-stock had been fought successfully; but the final victory was by no means gained. The enemy, driven from the open field, was firing from behind walls and ditches, not disdaining to form entrenchments of the most antiquated mud. Previous to their commencement of business, the directors of the London and Westminster applied to the committee of private bankers for admission to the Clearing House. This was refused. The directors also applied for permission to have a drawing account at the *Bank of England.*

This, too, was refused. But these were but small obstacles, and greater ones showed in front. Some shrewd entrepreneurs, in league with the enemy, discovered that the new joint-stock bank possessed no power of suing its debtors; and to remedy this serious evil a fresh campaign had to be undertaken.

On the 7th of May, 1834, just three months after they commenced business, the directors of the London and Westminster Bank applied by petition to the House of Commons for powers to sue and be sued. On the introduction of the bill granting such powers, the *Bank of England* was not ashamed to appear by counsel against it, notwithstanding which opposition it passed the House. Even this was not the last shot fired from behind the walls of Threadneedle Street In the ordinary course of business, bills of exchange were drawn upon the London and Westminster Bank from the country, and accepted, as a matter of course. The authorities of the *Bank of England* immediately gave notice to their new opponent, that by accepting bills they were *"infringing the privilege of the Bank."* Here was the opening of another mighty battle, accompanied by a marvelous fruitage for the lawyers.

The matter was dragged, with anticipated sluggishness, through all the courts of law and equity, and, in due course, made its attendance before the *Areopagus of the British Isles*. The Lords called in the support of the twelve judges, and after much high-feed—or high-fed—persuasiveness, the decision went in favour of Threadneedle Street. Four years' litigation, and the loss of as many thousand pounds, was the only misfortune experienced by the London and Westminster Bank in this struggle. The adverse decision of the Lords cost the bank not a single customer, the law being dodged, as usual, by a clever business apparatus.

All that was done was an arrangement with the country joint-stock banks to draw upon the London and Westminster Bank "without acceptance," in the same way as the Bank of

Ireland draws upon the *Bank of England*. In this case, as well as others, it is satisfactory to see that, in the battle between law and common sense, the latter infrequently fails in getting the upper hand. The principle of joint-stock banks was established in apparent defiance of an *Act of the House of Commons*, and the founders upheld their work in disobedience of a decision of the House of Lords.

Its infantile struggle overcome, the career of the London and Westminster Bank was one of unclouded prosperity. The first annual report, issued March 4, 1835, stated that the paid-up capital of the bank—increased by two calls of £5 each upon the shareholders—had risen from £50,000 to £244,945, while the business done was such as to allow a dividend of 4 percent. By the end of December, 1835, the number of shares issued had increased to 17,818. Soon afterwards the directors ordered a fourth call of £5 per share, payable the following April. This made £20 paid upon each share, the whole capital exceeding now £400,000. In 1836, the paid-up capital rose to above half a million; reaching £800,000 in 1842, and £1,000,000 in 1847.

It was in the latter year that the new joint-stock bank commenced its course of punitive justice by scoffing its old enemies, the private bankers. The first bank which was absorbed was the old firm of *Young and Son*, formerly *Weston and Young*, carrying on business in Southwark. The last victim, devoured in 1864, was the old-established firm of *Jones, Loyd, and Co*. The ancients of Lombard Street now began to tremble for their existence; and as they had formerly sneered at joint-stock banks, they now expressed their hatred with still greater cordiality. Though having risen in a few years to the position of the second greatest bank in the kingdom, the *London and Westminster* was unable to obtain admission to the *Clearing House*. Its portals were as jealously guarded as the entrance to those sacred regions—

"The Elysian plains, earth's farthest end, Where Rhadamanthus dwells."

Rhadamanthus, of Lombard Street, did not open the golden (or paper) gates of the *Elysii Campi* till the month of June, 1854, after more than twenty years' knocking at the door. An extra bonus of £80,000 to the prosperous shareholders of the London and Westminster proved the final sop to Cerberus.

# A TALE OF FORGERY

One of the dominant roots of the abrupt success of the *London and Westminster Bank*, or, in other words, of the principle of joint-stock banking, was the besmirched social position of many private bankers, particularly in the country. They availed themselves to the fullest extent of *the right, granted to them by the Legislature, of issuing small notes*, in not a few instances without the least solid cash foundation. By an astonishing glitch, the *Bank of England* was not allowed to issue a single one-pound note, while country bankers, many of whom were mere retail shop-keepers, deluged the provinces with millions.

The repeated failures of these so-called bankers, caused of necessity terrible suffering among the middle and the lower classes, who mostly held their worthless notes, and gave rise to more or less extensive financial crises. It was in vain that leading papers, such as the *Times*, lifted their voice against this unsound state of commercial legislation. "*If notes of that kind are to be circulated,*" argued the latter paper, "*the Bank of England ought to do it, not hovels in the country, dignified by the title of 'Bank' being written over a dairy or a cheese monger's shop.*"

Notwithstanding these and other expressions of public opinion, country banks continued to flourish, not a little owing to the support which they received from Thread-needle Street, where they were looked upon as trusty allies against the threatened invasion of joint-stock. But country bankers alone were not at fault, for among many of the London private bankers there obtained a low state of morality, during the first quarter of the present century. Failures were numerous, and frauds by no means rare.

One of the most extraordinary of these, and which created an intense sensation at the time, eclipsing for the moment all other public events, was that of *Henry Fauntleroy*, partner in the old banking house of *Marsh, Sibbald, & Co.*, of Berners Street.

The father of Henry Fauntleroy was originally clerk to a City banker, but on account of his thorough knowledge of banking, obtained a partnership in the firm of *Marsh, Sibbald, and Co.*, in 1792. On his death, in 1807, Henry Fauntleroy became his successor, and before long obtained a complete mastery over his partners, who willingly submitted to what they took for superior wisdom and energy. The business, from the first, was unfortunate. There was want of capital, and, what was worse, need of knowledge of even the first rudiments of banking; and the whole weight of the establishment fell upon Henry Fauntleroy, a young man of only twenty-two.

No wonder then that, before he had been long at the helm, the bank suffered a loss of £20,000, and after a three years' management, or mismanagement, on his part, the firm was found to have lost near £100,000. Extremely ambitious, and utterly devoid of honesty, Henry Fauntleroy did not for a moment think of making his position known; but, to hide the insolvency of the firm from his partners, as well as the public, he took to falsifying the books. This was so artfully done that it required subsequently the utmost keenness of the accountant, aware as he was of the forgeries, to detect the imposition.

The trouble to impose upon his partners, who had the complete confidence in him, was a comparatively easy one, and they actually took their business to be in the most prosperous condition, when it had been for years hopelessly bankrupt. The world, too, fancied Henry Fauntleroy to be an uncommonly prosperous as well as an honest man; and many were the signs of confidence bestowed upon him by his clients and friends.

Among others, he was appointed in 1814—after having been actually insolvent for more than four years—one of three trustees to a family named Young, consisting of eight children. There stood to the account of the family a very large sum in the Three percent, in the *Bank of England.*

Meanwhile, the firm of *Marsh, Sibbald, and Co.,* got involved deeper and deeper. Many an evening, after his partners and his clerks had retired from the bank, Henry Fauntleroy, when sitting down to his accustomed task of altering the balances of the house, felt faint and weary at the work, the fear of detection staring him in the face. But he was not the man to shrink from a labour which he had once undertaken, and having committed his forgeries, he invariably went forth into society, brimful of the spirit of enjoyment, the gayest of the gay.

Falsifying the accounts, however, was found to be, after a while, insufficient; Henry Fauntleroy urgently required some cash in hand, not to be had from the bank till. So he went a step further in his career. In May, 1815, a power of attorney was presented at the *Bank of England,* purporting to bear the signature of Francis Young, of Chichester, for the sale of £5,000 at three percent. The power was forged; nevertheless, it passed the ordeal of the Bank examinations, and the money-was paid.

From this period many powers, bearing the signature of Marsh and Co., as attorneys, were acted on by Henry Fauntleroy. Most of these were attested by two of the clerks of the banking house; and while some of them were to replace stock previously sold, others were to provide for different purposes. No suspicion appears to have been excited at the *Bank of England;* the mere knowledge that the power was given to a "highly respectable" banker was held to be quite sufficient not for a moment to doubt its genuineness. It is somewhat curious that the fact of private bankers publishing no accounts, so far from deducting from the trust reposed in them, seems to have acted formerly just in the contrary way. As a man who speaks little is often held to be wise, so a banker about whose fortune nothing whatever was known, was held of necessity to be immensely wealthy. It seems the tendency of mankind to believe in veiled prophets of Khorasan.

Henry Fauntleroy had been the leading head of the firm of Marsh and Co. for seventeen years—and bankrupt for fourteen—when the crash came at last. Some difficulties having arisen in the management of the trust of the Young family, Fauntleroy's brother trustees decided, much against his will, that the affair should be thrown into Chancery. This was in the spring of 1824. The Court, with unwonted rapidity, made an order that the whole of the property held in trust should, in the month of November, be paid over to the Accountant-General; which order was communicated, not to Fauntleroy, but to one of the other trustees.

The latter at once went to the *Bank of England*, and was panic-stricken at the discovery that the whole of the stock had been sold out without his knowledge. He lost no time in communicating with the second trustee, and it was decided to put the matter at once into the hands of the police. This hurried on the march of events. Early one morning in September, 1824, Plank, a Bow Street officer, accompanied by another mysterious-looking person with a packet under his arm, made his appearance at the banking house of Messrs. Marsh and Co., "Is Mr. Henry Fauntleroy within?" inquired the officer. "Yes," was the answer; "will you send in your name?"

Without vouchsafing a reply, the two strangers pushed forward, and, though the clerk made a desperate effort to prevent them entering the sanctum of his master, they soon found themselves in the presence of the banker. "You are Mr. Henry Fauntleroy?" "I am!" "I hold a warrant for your apprehension on the charge of forgery," exclaimed the Bow Street runner. A deadly pallor passed over the face of the banker;

his knees trembled under him, and he seemed ready to sink to the ground. "Good God, cannot this matter be settled" he hurriedly exclaimed.

Without replying, Plank's companion took handcuffs from under his arm, and securing his prisoner, led him to a hackney-coach waiting outside. They proceeded to the residence of Mr. Conant, the magistrate; and after an interview of the prisoner with one of his clerks, Freshfield, solicitor to the *Bank of England,* accompanied by Plank, proceeded to the banking house of Marsh and Co. to search the papers. The search was successful, in so far as documents unparalleled in the history of crime were discovered. It was found that Henry Fauntleroy had kept, among his other books, a regular and minute account of the forgeries he had committed, amounting to above £300,000.

At the bottom of the list was the following extraordinary acknowledgment, written in a clear, bold hand: — *"In order to keep up the credit of our house, I have forged powers of attorney, and have, thereupon, sold out all these sums, without the knowledge of any of my partners. I have given credit in the accounts for the interest when it became due. —* Henry Fauntleroy."

On the 30th of October, 1824, Henry Fauntleroy was accused at the Old Bailey for forging a power of attorney and other documents. The trial excited an intense interest among all classes of the community. "Hardly anything else," says a paper of the day, "is talked about." The bankers name was in every mouth; his portrait in every shop window. Henry Fauntleroy behaved with great bravery, if not insolence, at the trial, declaring that his crime had not been committed out of motives of personal gain, but from a "feeling of honour." It was not to save himself, but the bank in which he was a partner that he had become a forger.

Singularly enough, there were not a few persons who sympathized with the criminal in his position, and looked upon him almost as a hero. Among these were some men of wealth and influence, who made desperate efforts to save Henry Fauntleroy from the doom of the gallows. Class interest, or class prejudice, was stirred up—it seemed so dreadful to hang a banker. However, all these efforts availed nothing. The jury found the prisoner guilty, and — forgery encountering then the highest penalty of the law—he was led to execution on the 30th of November, 1824.

Never was there such a crowd seen at the foot of Newgate as on this cold autumn morning. More than a hundred thousand people occupied the ground, to the very roof of the houses, from Ludgate Hill to the farthest comer of Smithfield. The multitude, always doubting the fact that there is but one law for the rich as for the poor, evidently wished to make quite sure of a banker being executed for forgery; and the question asked from mouth to mouth was whether it was really the guilty great man who was led to the scaffold.

There could be no doubt the doomed man was really and truly Henry Fauntleroy, the banker. But he seemed dead already when led under the fatal drop. Guided, or carried, by two clergymen, one taking each arm, the unhappy man was scarcely able to drag himself to the fatal spot—his lips moved convulsively, his whole frame trembled; till in a few minutes justice was done upon earth. The death on the scaffold of Henry Fauntleroy had the force of a public event, and while it produced a lasting sensation, undermined, to a considerable extent, the faith in private banking.

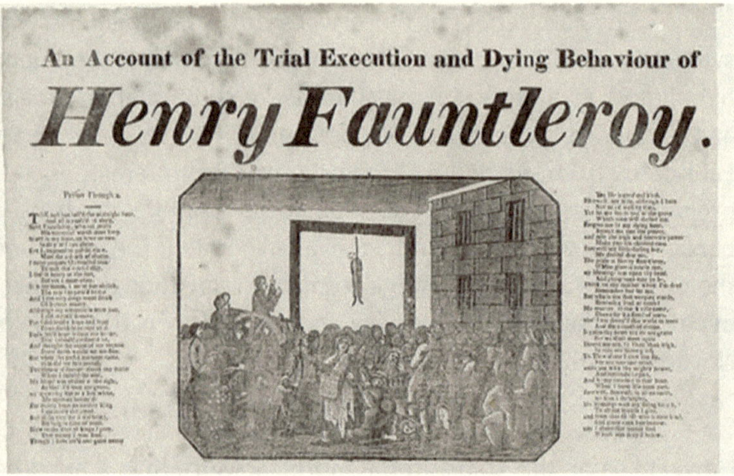
An Account of the Trial Execution and Dying Behaviour of

*Henry Fauntleroy.*

# A TRIO OF BILL-BROKERS.

Just before joint-stock banks came to overpower the trade of private banking, a small house in the eastern counties gave birth to a new financial organization, the growth of which, for a time, was almost more gigantic than that of joint-stock banking. It was in Norwich that arose the world-famous firm of **OVEREND & CO.,** the oldest house in existence that attempted *bill-brokering* in its contemporary form. The firm was a direct offshoot of the *Norwich Bank*, established by *Henry Gurney* in 1770.

The founder of the bank was succeeded by his son, *Bartlett Gurney*, who, in 1803, took into partnership his cousin, *John Gurney*, and several other members of the family. John Gurney had previously been a wool-stapler and spinner of beaten yarn. In this business, he became familiar with *Joseph Smith*, a most active and energetic man, largely engaged in the woolen trade, but giving much of his time to discounting bills, acting as a sort of intermediate agent between the Norwich bank and his own numerous friends and acquaintances.

The latter occupation was by far the most profitable of the two; and Joseph Smith was frank enough to communicate the fact to his most intimate associates. One evening, while discussing the interesting subject over a bottle of wine, the question was started: *"Why not establish a house solely devoted to the trade in bills?"* The suggestion came from *John Overend*, an enterprising young man, clerk to *Joseph Smith*. It was beneficially entertained on all sides, and the matter led to negotiations between the proprietors of the *Norwich Bank* and several of the leading merchants of the town.

Joseph Smith personally declined to connect himself with the proposed bill-dealing institution, but offered to give his advice and assistance; and it was finally determined to put forward three young men as founders of the firm— namely, *John Overend*; *Samuel Gurney*, twenty-one years of age, the second son of John Gurney, previously a clerk to Fry, who had married his sister, the celebrated Mrs. Fry; and *Thomas Richardson*, a clerk in the banking-house of *Smith, Wright, and Gray*, afterwards *Esdaile and Co.* These three young men, all clerks at the time, laid the basis of one of the most gigantic financial establishments of modern days.

The new establishment was, on the outset, a mere agency of the *Norwich Bank*, and under the entire superintendence of the *Gurney family*. But, for some reasons of their own, the latter thought it best not to show this patronage too openly, and the firm was brought forward under the title of *Richardson, Overend, and Co.* Richardson soon retired, when the house commenced trading as *Overend and Co.,* the name it taken, although Overend died not long after, leaving Samuel Gurney sole representative of the firm. It was he who raised the house to the distinguished position it subsequently occupied. The way in which this was accomplished has stamped the name of Samuel Gurney as one of the most eminent *financiers* of his time. While ordinary minds are able only to draw advantage from prosperity, to *"make hay while the sun shines,"* Gurney distilled honey out of thorns, and built a temple of wealth on a foundation of distress and adversity.

The panic of 1825 was remarkable for a distrust of bankers. Several London banks failed, and, according to Horsley Palmer, no fewer *than eighty private banks in the country; probably many more would have failed* but for the support they obtained from the *Bank of England.* In this crisis, Samuel Gurney came forward as the champion of *a new principle of banking.* He advocated that private bankers, particularly those of the metropolis, ought to change their mode of investment, and, instead of employing their surplus funds in the purchase of

Government securities, to be discounted at the *Bank of England,* place them on deposit with bill-brokers, so as to be independent of the Bank.

This, he argued, would prevent future financial crises, occasioned basically by the dependence of too many private houses upon a single banking institution. The advice was followed largely, and a great many London bankers, besides many houses in the country, began connecting themselves with bill-brokers. Almost the whole of this business fell to the share of *Overend and Co.*—that is, Samuel Gurney—who thus became the banker of many hundreds of private banks.

When the latter had any surplus funds, they placed them on deposit with Overend & Co., and when required, they withdrew them from Overend & Co. This arrangement made the private bankers directly independent of the *Bank of England,* releasing them from an accessory not unfrequently fraught with danger, and at all times with impediments for free action. The change was accomplished in a few years. *George Carr Glyn*, when examined before the Bank Charter Committee, in 1832, speaking for the London bankers generally, said: "*We do not feel the slightest dependence upon the Bank of England, nor do we feel the slightest obligation to it in any way.*"

The immense success of the new firm of bill-brokers could not fail to call up rivals. The first of them, in point of time, was the house of *Sanderson and Co.* Sanderson, the founder of the firm, was originally a clerk, or manager, with Overend and Co., and on getting considerable experience in the business, had sufficient courage to set up on his own account. He acquired wealth, became a Member of Parliament, married the daughter of a nobleman, and—probable consequence of the latter "*interesting event*"—stopped payment in 1847. But he succeeded, after a while, in paying off all his creditors, and started afresh, taking into partnership Sandeman, a wealthy, or supposed wealthy, stock-broker.

The new firm had a brilliant career of about nine years, and then, in 1857, again stopped payment. This time the very extensive business was wound up under the inspection of three of the largest creditors, of whom two were private bankers. It turned out, on investigation, that the total liabilities amounted to the enormous sum of £5,442,285 only a portion of which was secured by bills of exchange. Once more the giant rose from the ground, but after a short season of business, was fairly extinguished, and absorbed by a new joint-stock association—the Consolidated Discount Company, which started with a capital of one million, and a promise of 10 percent, to the shareholders.

The fall of Sanderson and Co., raised the position of another great firm of bill-brokers, third in time, but second in magnitude. This was the house of *Alexander and Co.*, established by Alexander, chief clerk in the private bank of *Robarts, Curtis, and Co.*

An idea may be formed of the vast transactions of the above three bill-dealing firms—including the house now bankrupt—from a statement of Mr. Neave, a well-known authority, given in evidence before the Select Committee of the House of Commons on the Bank Acts, which sat in 1858. Neave states that, a short time before this period, about 1856, there were three bill-brokers in London holding deposits to the extent of fifteen million and a half sterling.

He does not give the name of these brokers; but Mr. J. W. Gilbart, in his *"Logic of Banking,"* supplies the deficiency as follows: —

| 1 | Overend, Gurney, and Co | £8,000,000 |
| 2 | Alexander and Co., | £4,000,000 |
| 3 | Sandeman and Co., | £3,500,000 |
| | Total | £15,500,000 |

Considering that each of the above three firms had grown up within little more than a quarter of a century, and that all of them were founded by men not possessed of wealth, and in the social position of clerks, the figures tell a tale nothing less than marvelous. Later, joint-stock has invaded the domain of the bill-brokers no less than that of ordinary bankers.

The *National Discount Company* and the *London Discount Company* were the first to start in the footsteps of the Gurneys and Alexanders; and other joint-stock companies, within the last few years, have followed in the same direction. It was probably in expectation of this rivalry that Samuel Gurney expressed himself so severely against the principle of joint-stock association, when cited as a witness before the Parliamentary committee on joint-stock banks, in 1836.

It was the opinion of the great bill-broker that *"the peculiar distinction"* of joint-stock banks consisted in being *"neither legitimate nor respectable,"* and that, moreover, the system was *"dangerous and requiring regulation."* And when the Chairman, the Chancellor of the Exchequer, inquired of Gurney, *"Do you conceive it would be an improvement or a disadvantage to the present system if joint-stock banks were permitted to be established with a limited liability?"* Gurney replied, probably with some emphasis, *"I think it would be a very serious addition to the evils of the case."*

In the twenty years following his examination before the Parliamentary Committee, Samuel Gurney must have suffered much, not only in seeing joint-stock get the upper hand over private banking, but accompanied by the greatest of "evils," the "limited liability." Gurney died in 1856, and was succeeded by David Barclay Chapman, who retired from the firm on the 21st December, 1857.

Share certificate of Overend, Gurney and Co.

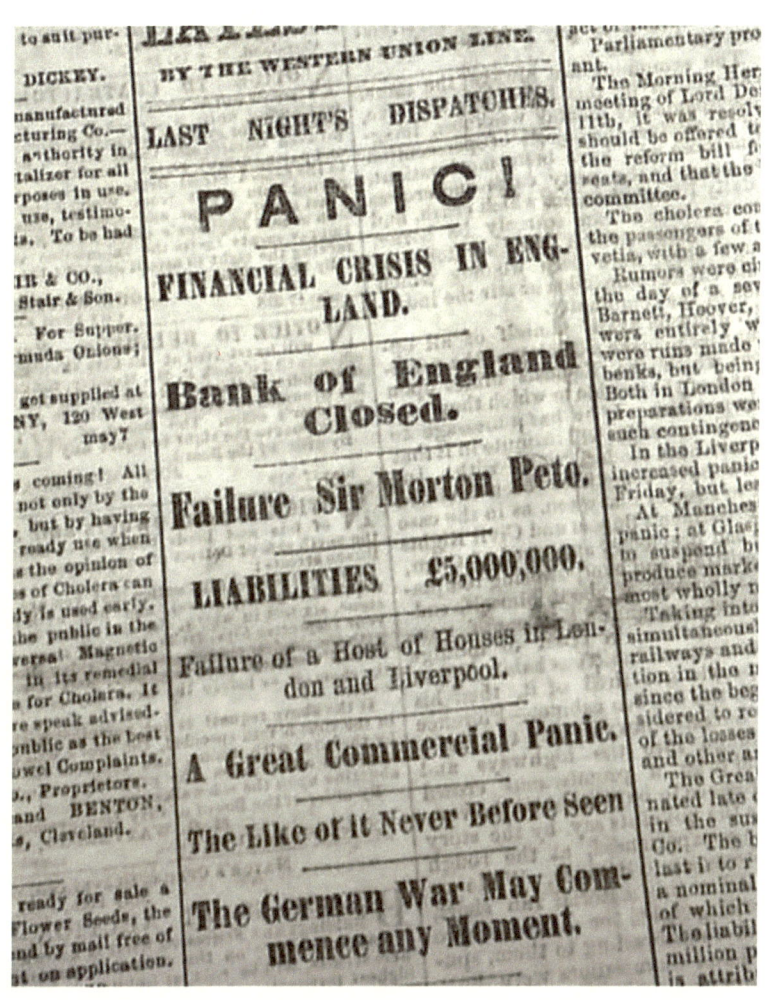

**THE END**